Living by the Word

Living by the Word

Joel S. Goldsmith

Edited By
Lorraine Sinkler

Acropolis Books, Publisher
Atlanta, Georgia

For information contact:
ACROPOLIS BOOKS, INC.
Atlanta, Georgia

www.acropolisbooks.com

Library of Congress Cataloging-in-Publication Data

Goldsmith, Joel S., 1892 - 1964.
    Living by the Word / Joel S. Goldsmith ; edited by Lorraine Sinkler.
        p. cm.
    Includes bibliographical references.
    ISBN 1-889051-60-8 (pbk. : alk. paper)
    1. Spiritual life--Biblical teaching. I. Sinkler, Lorraine. II. Title.

BP610 .G641585 2002
299'.93--dc21
                                              2002023234

Except the Lord build the house,
they labour in vain that build it. . .

– Psalm 127

"Illumination dissolves all material ties and binds men together with the golden chains of spiritual understanding; it acknowledges only the leadership of the Christ; it has no ritual or rule but the divine, impersonal universal Love; no other worship than the inner Flame that is ever lit at the shrine of Spirit. This union is the free state of spiritual brotherhood. The only restraint is the discipline of Soul; therefore, we know liberty without license; we are a united universe without physical limits, a divine service to God without ceremony or creed. The illumined walk without fear – by Grace."

–*The Infinite Way* by Joel S. Goldsmith

Dedication

Twentieth century mystic Joel S. Goldsmith revealed to the Western world the nature and substance of mystical living that demonstrated how mankind can live in the consciousness of God. The clarity and insight of his teachings, called the Infinite Way, were captured in more than thirty-five books and in over twelve hundred hours of tape recordings that, today, perpetuate his message.

Joel faithfully arranged to have prepared from his class tapes, monthly letters which were made available as one of the most important tools to assist students in their study and application of the Infinite Way teachings. He felt each of these letters came from an ever-new insight that would produce a deeper level of understanding and awareness of truth as students worked diligently with this fresh and timely material.

Each yearly compilation of the *Letters* focused on a central theme, and it became apparent that working with an entire year's material built an ascending level of consciousness. The *Letters* were subsequently published as books, each containing all the year's letters. The publications became immensely popular as they proved to be of great assistance in the individual student's development of spiritual awareness.

Starting in 1954, the monthly letters were made availiable to students wishing to subscribe to them. Each year of the *Letters* was published individually during 1954 through 1959 and made available in book form. From 1960 through 1970 the *Letters* were published and renamed as books with the titles:

1960 Letters	*Our Spiritual Resources*
1961 Letters	*The Contemplative Life*
1962 Letters	*Man Was Not Born to Cry*
1963 Letters	*Living Now*
1964 Letters	*Realization of Oneness*
1965 Letters	*Beyond Words and Thoughts*
1966 Letters	*The Mystical I*
1967 Letters	*Living Between Two Worlds*
1968 Letters	*The Altitude of Prayer*
1969 Letters	*Consciousness Is What I Am*
1970 Letters	*Awakening Mystical Consciousness*

Joel worked closely with his editor, Lorraine Sinlker, to ensure each letter carried the continuity, integrity, and pure consciousness of the message. After Joel's transition in 1964, Emma A. Goldsmith (Joel's wife) requested that Lorraine continue working with the monthly letters, drawing as in the past from the inexhaustible tape recordings of his class work with students. The invaluable work by Lorraine and Emma has ensured that this message will be preserved and available in written form for future generations. Acropolis Books is honored and privileged to offer in book form the next eleven years of Joel's teaching.

The 1971 through 1981 *Letters* also carry a central theme for each year, and have been renamed with the following titles:

1971 Letters	*Living by the Word*
1972 Letters	*Living the Illumined Life*
1973 Letters	*Seek Ye First*
1974 Letters	*Spiritual Discernment: the Healing Consciousness*
1975 Letters	*A Message for the Ages*
1976 Letters	*I Stand on Holy Ground*
1977 Letters	*The Art of Spiritual Living*
1978 Letters	*God Formed Us for His Glory*
1979 Letters	*The Journey Back to the Father's House*
1980 Letters	*Showing Forth the Presence of God*
1981 Letters	*The Only Freedom*

Acropolis Books dedicates this series of eleven books to Lorraine Sinkler and Emma A. Goldsmith for their ongoing commitment of ensuring that these teachings will never be lost to the world.

Table of Contents

Living by the Word

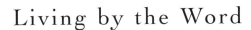

Chapter One

Living by the Word

There comes a certain moment in the experience of every person when a touch of the Spirit breaks through into consciousness, when a ray of light penetrates, not because of him, but in spite of him. From the moment that ray touches him, the end is inevitable: he is going to find his way to the very center of his being, right to the throne of God.

For some, the way is long and difficult because of the many facets of humanhood which have been built up and from which we cannot free ourselves. We do not find it easy to let go of many of the qualities which hold us back; and I am not thinking only of the evil qualities. Some of the good ones, too, are positive deterrents to our spiritual progress.

As this ray of light continues to penetrate, it pushes us, it leads us, even to the point of stumbling. We have periods of gradual growth toward spiritual consciousness, and then all of a sudden we get a wallop that sets us back about ten degrees, and we have to pick ourselves up and begin all over again. That happens to everybody on this path, who, like most of us, yields reluctantly to the spiritual impulse.

There are a few gifted individuals who, before this present

experience on earth, have been so wonderfully prepared that their way seems to be much easier than ours. They seem to perceive spiritual light quickly, and their progress appears always to be onward and upward.

In that purity of consciousness, the childlike consciousness, which many adults have brought over with them from their previous development, the ascent into spiritual consciousness is a beautiful one, gradual and harmonious, and beset with very few problems, and even those few not of their own making but having to do mostly with their families, friends, and that which they have picked up on the journey.

For most people, however, the path is up and down, and usually there comes the realization at the end of a year or two, and possibly at the end of every year or two, "Well, I am a trace ahead of where I was last year or two years ago."

The Promises of Scripture Are Given to the Children of God

Throughout scripture, there are comforting promises to aid us on our journey, such as:

> God is our refuge and strength,
> a very present help in trouble.
>
> Psalm 46:1

> Fear thou not; for I am with thee: be not dismayed;
> for I am thy God: I will strengthen thee; yea,
> I will help thee; yea, I will uphold thee with
> the right hand of my righteousness....

> For I the Lord thy God will hold thy right hand,
> saying unto thee, Fear not; I will help thee.
>
> Isaiah 41:10, 13

When thou passest through the waters,
I will be with thee; and through
the rivers, they shall not overflow thee:
when thou walkest through the fire,
thou shalt not be burned; neither shall
the flame kindle upon thee.

Isaiah 43:2

Behold, I give unto you power to tread on serpents
and scorpions, and over all the power of the enemy:
and nothing shall by any means hurt you.

Luke 10:19

I will never leave thee, nor forsake thee.

Hebrews 13:5

Whenever we come to a spiritual promise in scripture, a divine promise of safety, security, peace, health, wholeness, or harmony, we should realize that it is not a human being making promises or delivering a message. It is the Christ Itself, the spirit of God in man, not merely a man reporting what God said. It is the voice of the Christ Itself saying to us, "I will never leave thee, nor forsake thee," and when an individual is attuned to God, these impartations come.

It is important to remember that just because the Bible is filled with spiritual promises, we must not think that they apply to you or to me as human beings. No spiritual promise applies to a human being, or human beings would all be saved. They apply to you and me when we are in our spiritual oneness with God and are no longer human beings, but have become the sons of God. It is when we make our contact with the Infinite Invisible that we become children of God.

> For what man knoweth the things of a man, save the
> spirit of man which is in him? even so the things of
> God knoweth no man, but the Spirit of God.
> I Corinthians 2:11

> But ye are not in the flesh, but in the Spirit, if so be
> that the Spirit of God dwell in you.
> Romans 8:9

The whole message of the Infinite Way is teaching us to make that contact with God. It is not trying to give us a new religion or present a new message from some human being about something. It is not trying to invent a new way of healing the sick and feeding the hungry. The whole import of the message of the Infinite Way is, through writings, lectures, classes, and recordings, to lift us to a state of spiritual apprehension, wherein and whereby we become the sons of God.

When we then have a divine impartation from within, we are not human beings; we are children of God, consciously one with the Father. Until that time comes, we are "man, whose breath is in his nostrils: for wherein is he to be accounted of?"[1] Who is going to worry about mortal man? Not even God bothers to save mortal man. God lets him rot away on battlefields or in prison dungeons, or wherever he finds himself.

It is only the son of God, the spiritual image and likeness of God, who is held in the bosom of the Father, and in order to achieve that relationship, we have to make the return journey from that banquet with "the swine,"[2] just as the Prodigal did. We have to leave behind all the thoughts, people, and doings of that swine-ish world and return to the Father, abandoning even mother and father and sister and brother for His name's sake. We have to abandon all our previous concepts of life, and not only previous concepts of sin, but previous concepts of what constitutes good.

The Bible, the Record of Man's Struggles and Aspirations

Let us understand that these promises that are in scripture apply to us, not because of our voicing or repeating them as affirmations: they apply to us in proportion as we make our conscious contact with the Infinite Invisible and receive them as impartations from within. Every divine promise in scripture is the Christ uttering Itself, and whoever hears It receives not only the benefit for himself, but for all those who are in his charge.

Whether the Hebrew prophets were instructing the Israelites under them in a moral code, whether they were guiding them out of Egypt through the Red Sea, or whether those prophets were engaged in the rebuilding of the temples, whoever the divinely inspired leader was at any given time, he was given the responsibility of caring for his people. They had to be rebuked and they had to be disciplined because they were still trying at times to break away and return to Baal and mingle with the heathens. They were going through the preliminary stages of initiatehood, and all of us when we are in this stage of initiation, that is, when we are in the stage of passing from humanhood to the realization of our divinity, must be admonished. We are all given the Ten Commandments; we are all given clear warnings of disaster if we do not change and turn from our human ways.

> For I have no pleasure in the death of him
> that dieth, saith the Lord God: wherefore
> turn yourselves, and live ye.
> Ezekiel 18:32

Some of these prophets, sages, and seers gave way to fear, doubt, and discouragement as did both the Psalmist and the Master when they cried, "My God, my God, why hast thou forsaken me?"[3] Actually, that cry of despair from the Master may or may not have been uttered. There was Jesus, suspended high above the heads of those around him, undoubtedly in a weakened state. It does not seem likely that those down on the ground could have heard the words that he uttered because it does not seem that in that state he could have called out in a very loud voice. So there is a serious doubt that comes into my mind as to whether or not he ever spoke such words since he well knew the nature of his demonstration.

If he did and if those were his words, they represented a momentary fear, a momentary lapse, due to the actual fact of the Crucifixion. It may well have been that in his mind there was some thought of a miraculous deliverance from the experience, and then, finding it necessary to go through with it, there could have been that momentary sense of fear or doubt. On the other hand, it could also have been a mistranslation of what was uttered. He could very well have said something that sounded like that and which later was translated incorrectly.

The point, however, is not whether or not he made that statement, but rather the fact that probably every religious leader all through the ages has at times experienced doubt, fear, wonder, or discouragement. The Bible is the record of human aspirations and man's emergence into spiritual realization. It is the record of our own struggles, alternating between hope and despair. Those outcries of despair might have been uttered by you or me while we are on the path and have not fully attained.

The Difficulties of Leading
Human Consciousness Out of Itself

Always there will be questions in our mind whether we are doing the right thing in accord with God's plan. We know our motives are right; we want to do right; our desires are right; but still we are not certain. Is this God's plan? Should we be doing what we are doing today? If we were hearing God correctly, would there be something else for us to be doing at this very moment? Always that question comes to us, and more especially does it come to those who are practitioners, teachers, or group leaders, to those who are responsible for the spiritual unfoldment of students who have entrusted themselves to the teacher or teaching, because then one is not merely responsible for one's own demonstration, but for those who have come to him to be guided along the Path.

If Moses alone had been involved, it would have been an easy thing for him to have failed or to have succeeded since he would have had only his own experience to consider. But he had those hordes of Hebrews, people who were in slavery, whom he had been directed to lead into freedom. And what happened? While under his guidance, over and over again they complained, "Would to God we had died by the hand of the Lord in the land of Egypt, when we sat by the flesh pots, and when we did eat bread to the full; for ye have brought us forth into this wilderness, to kill this whole assembly with hunger."[4] They had been slaves, but at least they had had food in their stomachs and a place to sleep.

How true it is even today that "man, whose breath is in his nostrils" will always choose to be a slave if only someone will assure him of a couple of meals a day and a place to sleep. It does not even have to be a good place or good food. Just so long as he does not have the personal responsibility of going out and earning it or competing for it, he is perfectly willing to sign away his vote to whoever will provide that little meager living. That is human nature.

The Hebrews did not have the vision of Moses, and they pleaded to go back into slavery so they would be fed, housed, and clothed. Their leader knew he had a hard task asked of him because they might have to go without food, without housing, and they might have to go through many dangers. But in spite of that he knew that if they would stick, they would be led into their ultimate freedom from slavery, and so he had to fight the very people whom he was trying to set free.

The experience of Moses was repeated by Elijah, Isaiah, Jesus, John, and Paul. All those leaders had to battle the very people they were trying to bless. Why? Because those whom they were trying to bless were going to be called upon for sacrifices which they themselves did not want to make. They wanted their way, and they not only wanted their way but they wanted it right then and there. People have been perfectly willing at every stage in history to forego a future good for a present half-good.

Is it surprising that the Hebrew prophets and Jesus, Paul, Peter, and John had moments of wondering if it was worthwhile, and if they were interpreting God's message correctly, since they seemed to be the only ones who had faith in it? Even these great leaders retained a trace of humanhood, and that expressed itself at some time or other in doubt, fear, and discouragement.

Do We or Do We Not Entertain a Sense of Separation from God?

Every time we are touched with doubt, fear, limitation, or a sense of discouragement, let us acknowledge that what is operating in our consciousness at that particular moment is a sense of separation from God. It is not a separation from God, because we cannot be separated from God. Why? Because there is no *we*. There is no such thing, actually, in all the world as you or me. God being infinite, God is all there is. God constitutes you and me; God constitutes our being. God is the essence of our being: the life, soul, mind, spirit, the law, the continuity, and the activity. God is the all in all of our individual being whether we be saint or sinner.

The degree of our sainthood is totally dependent upon the degree of our conscious realization of that oneness. The degree of our sinning capacity is the degree of the sense of separation that is set up within us. As a matter of fact, all there is to humanhood is the sense of separation from God.

We are not human beings as we seem to be: we are pure spiritual being. That which is called the Prodigal-experience or the Fall of Man, the Adam-and-Eve-experience, does not constitute separation. Adam and Eve before the Fall were also Adam and Eve after the Fall.

The moment that sense of separation begins to disappear, Christhood or divine sonship begins to be revealed. The whole thing takes place within ourselves. All this has nothing to do with God: this has to do with us. Do we or do we not entertain a sense of separation from God? Are we or are we not beginning to attain the realization of our spiritual sonship?

God is; God already is; but the part that God plays in our demonstration is this: were it not for the grace of God, we could not even be reaching out toward the realization of divine sonship. In other words, let no one ever take credit for being on the spiritual path because he did not bring himself there. No human being ever has and no human being ever will. It is the nature of a human being to love the company of swine. It is the nature of the human being to love degradation, separation from good, self-indulgence.

Be Still and Let the Word Well Up from Within

Let us not believe that the promises of Scripture are meant for human beings walking around living a purely human materialistic life. These divine promises are meant for us individually in proportion as we make our contact with God and receive those promises from within our own being. If it flashes into our mind, "This is my beloved Son, in whom I am well pleased,"[5] that is a divine promise, and we can rely on that. It is better than a note from the Bank of England. When we receive such an impartation from within, it will never leave us or forsake us, and it will always bring us back to the throne of God.

Once we hear in our ear, "Fear thou not, for I am with thee," that is all we need. That is as absolute an assurance of God's grace as was David's. We have attained God's grace when we have heard the "still small voice"[6] within us. Whether we have heard it as a voice or felt it as an impulse or just achieved it as an awareness, regardless of how it comes, we have attained God's grace. Then, we can say with confidence, "Oh well, He will lead me 'beside the still waters,'[7] even if I have to cross a few rough ones to get there. 'He maketh me to lie down in green pastures,'[7] even if I walk through a few barren ones before I arrive there."

The important point is not whether or not we have what we think of as complete happiness or peace today. As a rule, that is just some namby-pamby idea of what constitutes happiness or peace. What counts is whether or not we are preparing ourselves by study, by meditation, by companioning with those on the spiritual path for the hearing of that "still small voice," for the actual experience of the Christ.

Once we achieve it, we are free from organization, from governmental support, and from all those bonds that the human mind wants to place on itself. Once we have achieved this contact with our inner being, with our Christhood, we are in bondage to no man, to no organization, to no government, to no form of economy. We are then free in Christ, and we can say, "Christ lives my life. It makes no difference whether we have capitalism or communism; it makes no difference whether we have depressions or booms; it makes no difference whether we have floods or droughts. The Christ lives my life."

With Illumination, Concern Begins to Disappear

The secret is making the contact with the Infinite Invisible. Even after having achieved it, let us not be too disturbed if once in a while a sense of fear or discouragement comes in. Upon investigation, we usually find that that has not come through anything that has to do with our personal demonstration except inasmuch as our personal demonstration is affected by those around us. When these fears and doubts and hesitations come, it will probably be because of some friend, relative, patient, student, or somebody other than ourselves, and it is his demonstration that we are more concerned about than our own.

Nobody ever achieves spiritual leadership who has any concern for his own demonstration. No one ever achieves spiritual leadership while it makes any difference to him whether he eats or does not eat, whether he sleeps in a barn or in a house, whether he stays up all night or up all day, or whether he does this or that. As long as there is a personal concern or the need for personal demonstration, no one can ever achieve spiritual leadership.

All those who attain illumination and spiritual leadership and still have concern do not have it for their own well-being. Their particular fate means nothing to them. They are not concerned with their personal health or personal well-being, but rather with that of those who come within range of their consciousness or who look to them for guidance.

The Mystery of Godliness

As we study scripture, let us remember that there is no disgrace in coming to those moments of fear or doubt, but let us get over with them in a hurry and get back on the beam. Inwardly, we do know that there is not God and man: there is only God manifested and expressed as your individual being and mine. There is only God appearing on earth. "Great is the mystery of godliness: God was manifest in the flesh."[8] That is the mystery of godliness; God manifest in flesh, God appearing as individual being. There is no separation between God and Its own selfhood individually formed, but we can set up a sense of separation and that is what we are on the spiritual path to break down.

God has given us a body, and that body is this body. We will never be separated from this body because this body is the product of our consciousness. This body is our consciousness made manifest, expressed. The only way this sense of body can improve is for our consciousness of truth to improve or be enlarged, until we come to the place where there is no more our consciousness *and* God-consciousness, but where God-consciousness becomes solely and completely our consciousness. Then, of course, the body will show forth what the Master's body showed forth at the time of the ascension: pure spiritual being.

Until our consciousness is divested of all human theories and beliefs, our body will continue to show forth some good and some evil. This body improves in appearance in proportion as our spiritual discernment increases.

On this spiritual path, we are engaged in the work of "dying" daily. That "dying" daily consists of the falling away of the human, material, or mortal beliefs, and in proportion as they disappear our consciousness is that much more the clear transparency of God-consciousness. Therefore, our body, our business, and our home will take on a healthier, happier, and more prosperous appearance.

Evidences of Christ-Consciousness

Christ-consciousness, or God-consciousness, is achieved in proportion as we understand the nothingness of what is appearing out here as the discords of human existence, and it is in the attainment of that consciousness that the healing works take place, not only the healing of our own affairs, but of the whole world that comes within range of our consciousness. If we understood that consciousness and body were one, inseparable and indivisible, so that there could be no danger either to consciousness or body, and that all the error being presented to our sight, hearing, taste, touch, and smell is but the result of universal human belief and is not actually a physical entity but a mental image in thought, we would have no fear of it. And in that lack of fear would be our degree of spiritual consciousness. That would be the overcoming.

How much evidence of hate, fear, or love of evil do we find in the life of Jesus Christ? It was the absence of any hate or love of evil that was his state of consciousness. And that is what constitutes Christ-consciousness.

In our individual experience, we attain Christ-consciousness by degrees. We attain It and we achieve It in a measure, not necessarily fully, but at least we do know that as we no longer hate error, fear it, battle it, or love it, in that degree we have attained Christ-consciousness, and that Consciousness is the one that dispels sin, disease, death, lack, and limitation for those who bring themselves to the activity of our consciousness.

We can never bless this world, never bless anyone or any group, while we are hating or fearing or loving the same evils that the world hates, fears, and loves. Our only degree of help is in proportion as we give up our hate and fear of this world and refrain from the battles of this world.

We show our Christ-consciousness in the degree that we can sit with the multitudes and let the multitudes come to us and draw of that light which we are, let the world come and draw upon our lack of fear, hate, and love of error. We prove the degree of our Christhood in the degree that we can see through the sin, hate, and fear of the world and not let them touch us.

Receiving the Word

There is a tremendous power in the consciousness of any individual who so attains this inner union as to receive these impartations of spiritual promises. And by bringing ourselves to those who have attained some measure of that, we partake in a measure of their Grace. "I, if I be lifted up from the earth, will draw all men unto me,"[9] unto that same level of consciousness.

We benefit by the realized Grace of one another. Whatever degree of Grace you and I attain, we share with each other and find it multiplied among ourselves. "For where two or three are gathered together in my name"[10]—in this same consciousness— there is this power felt in even a greater degree. That is why we must be vigilant to keep out of our consciousness the world's loves and hates, its fears and doubts, in order that as we come together this inflow of the Spirit can find itself multiplied on earth. Then, not only are we individually and collectively a blessing to all around us, but to all those in far places who, in some way or other, have been led to reach out and touch our consciousness. Never think for a moment that these people find our consciousness by any human means. They are spiritually directed from within and they reach out from all over the world just as we reach out all over the world to those who have illumination, and we find ourselves brought together, one with God.

Mere reading of the Bible and knowing and affirming the truths set forth in scripture is not too effectual. That is not because it is not truth: it is because it is truth known only with the mind without having come forth from an inner contact.

The declarations of the truths of scripture made with the mind serve as reminders of the truth of being in order that we may ultimately be led back to the actual contact itself. But they are ineffectual if they stop at the intellectual level and have not been dwelt upon until they bring us back to that inner contact whereby we actually receive the divine impartations from within. It is that divine impartation from within that is the word of God that comes with power, quick, sharp, powerful, guiding us unto the very Spirit. So, it is the word of God within us that is spoken to us, uttered within us, felt within us, achieved within us, that divine impulse recognized and realized that is the power in the world, and that it is that goes out and does the work of blessing. The healer of the world is Christ realized.

God's Gift of Gifts

Spiritual harmony is a gift of God. How are we to accept a gift of God except in that inner stillness in which we receive the divine impartation or gift? It is not something we can create; it is not something that anyone else can create for us. It is a spiritual gift of God to us through the word of God which we receive in the silence, in communion, in prayer, in a conscious at-one-ment with our Source through our mediator, our spiritual Selfhood, the divine part of us.

"Greater is he that is in you, than he that is in the world."[11] Is there any He within me other than my Self? Is there a "me" and somebody else in me? Of course not! I and my Self, alone in God. Therefore, the He that is within me is this mediator, this spiritual son of God which was planted in me from the beginning of time, and in everyone. This is the source through which we hear that Word, receive that guidance, receive that gift of God which is spiritual harmony made manifest as health, abundance, happy human relationships, and peace on earth.

I am with you. *I* will never leave you.
I was with you "before Abraham was."
I will be with you to the end of the world.
Take no thought for your life,
for *I* in the midst of you am with you.*

This has been thundered to us from within down through all the centuries, and we have been playing out here with baubles,

---

* Spontaneous meditations came to Joel during periods of uplifted consciousness and are not in any sense intended to be used as affirmations, denials, or formulas. They have been inserted from time to time to serve as examples of the free flowing of the Spirit. As the reader practices the Presence, he, too, in exalted moments, will receive ever new and fresh inspiration as the outpouring of the Spirit. –Ed.

unable to hear the "still small voice," even when it did thunder.

Life is a gift of God to us, and we can be assured that God will not take back that gift. We have no life except the one that we received by the grace of God. It is a gift of God; it is eternally ours, and we need never fear that we will lose that life.

Infinite abundance is ours. We need not earn it or deserve it. It is ours, because it is the gift of God. When we acknowledge that the riches of this earth are here for the benefit of mankind as a gift of God, we begin to realize the flow of that infinite abundance. We have dammed it up by looking to parents, brothers or sisters, or other relatives. Eventually, when all these have been exhausted, we begin looking to our children. We have so many places to look to avoid looking in the right place, within ourselves where God has established His kingdom in Its fullness. But that fullness begins to flow the moment we withdraw our gaze from some human source and begin to abide at the center of our being, dwelling there in the assurance that as our life is the gift of God, so is everything necessary to maintain and sustain that life a gift of God.

The word of God comes to us within ourselves through the attentive ear. Hearing the Word spoken through the mediator, "*I* in the midst of you am mighty, *I* will never leave you or forsake you. *I* will be with you to the end of the world," we have every right to act as if we were not dependent on any person in all this world, as if every moment we were consciously one with God, and we can receive the gift of God by turning within to that center where it is revealed to us through the word of God.

Heretofore, we may have lived primarily by human modes and means, with just a little recourse to God. Henceforth, if we abide on the spiritual path, we will live principally by means of the word of God which we hear in our meditations, and only incidentally on the outer plane through the added things.

Across the Desk

Just as with every New Year the world is flooded with pre-dictions about the year to come, so for many years it was Joel's custom to give students a special message for the New Year. This message was not one of prophecy, but of how to live effectively in the present moment. Each moment is to be looked upon as an opportunity to "turn ye, and live," because in that moment of turning, not only a new year, but a new life opens.

Most of these messages of Joel for the New Year have been incorporated in the writings. Your year—your life—can change if you will study and take seriously some of these chapters such as:

"The Spiritual New Year," *Man Was Not Born to Cry*

"Living Now," *Living Now*

"Consciousness Unfolding As the Harmony of the New Year," *Awakening Mystical Consciousness*

Chapter Two

Spiritual Discernment
of the Bible

The Bible, which is given to us as the word of spiritual wisdom, as revelations concerning the kingdom of God, must be spiritually discerned, but today even twenty centuries after the time of the Master, some religionists are still trying to interpret this hidden word of the kingdom literally, and, of course, are failing.

There is a spiritual kingdom. There is also the son of God who spiritually discerns the nature of this kingdom, the things of God, the laws of God, and who knows how to live a God-centered life. This kingdom can never be entered with the human mind or human body. It must be spiritually discerned.

If the kingdom of God were attained, if the things of God were understood, and if God were known aright, there would be none of the evils so evident on every hand: none of the sins, none of man's inhumanity to man, none of the diseases. All this would be wiped out in the understanding of God, because the understanding of God would leave no trace of sin or disease.

Letting Go of the Man of Earth

The statement, "My kingdom is not of this world,"[1] sets

forth very clearly that there is a difference between *"My* kingdom" and "this world." Later, Paul revealed that there are two men: There is the son of God, and there is "the natural man [who] receiveth not the things of the spirit of God: for they are foolishness unto him: neither can he know them, because they are spiritually discerned."[2] "The natural man" does not have the ability to discern spiritually.

And so it is that we are living partly in the world of sense, "this world," and partly in the kingdom of God, but certainly those of us who are on the path are striving to "die" to our humanhood, to "the creature,"[3] to "the natural man," in order that we may be reborn spiritually as children of God with spiritual discernment.

To all sincere seekers, the question arises: Is there a way for us to drop the man of earth? Can we "die" to it? Can we be reborn of the Spirit? Can we drop "the natural man" who does not receive the things of God, the blessings of God, the healings of God, and the grace of God, and can we become the children of God who are "heirs of God and joint-heirs?"[4]

If we believe in the mission of the Master, Christ Jesus, we must accept that as a possibility because it was to this end that the Master came among us and taught. He came to fishermen and told them to leave their "nets"[5]; he came to the men of earth and told them to leave their sins and their diseases. He showed them what to do and how to do it. Because of this, we know that even if we begin life as this man of earth, "the natural man," "this creature," we can at some time or other drop the mortal sense of existence—the physical, finite sense—and attain Christ-consciousness, spiritual awareness, the discernment of the things of God.

The Kingdom Is Revealed Through Meditation

The Master gives us a passage of scripture which may well start us on our spiritual journey, but we will need to remember consciously this passage at least once every day as we go into a meditation:

The kingdom of God cometh not with observation:

Neither shall they say,
Lo here! or Lo there! for behold,
the kingdom of God is within you.

Luke 17:20,21

Finding the kingdom of God is not going to be accomplished by going any place, because the kingdom of God is within us. There are those who believe that these words were addressed to the immediate followers of Jesus, but I think that few of us would like to believe this, because if so, it would have been only the Hebrews of Jesus' day who had the kingdom of God dwelling within them. We, however, have accepted the word of the Master as universal truth, truth that existed even "before Abraham was,"[6] truth that will exist until the end of the world, and so we believe that every word of the Master was meant for all those who had lived for centuries before him and for all those who will live unto the end of time.

To begin with, we acknowledge that that which we are seeking is already within us, and we must find it there. In our search for truth, we must turn within for the attainment of the kingdom of God. Many of us have already discovered, and more will eventually discover, that the kingdom of God is revealed through the practice of meditation or inner contemplation. The kingdom of God is within, and it is necessary, therefore, to go within that this kingdom may be revealed and that the spiritual faculty of discernment may be developed. At every step of our inward journey, the Master points out the way.

Admitting God Into Our Consciousness

As we close our eyes and turn within, we leave the world outside alone; we leave outside everything that has to do with family, business, profession, health, or wealth. We leave outside the good things and the bad things. We shut out the pictures of sense and call to remembrance this passage of the Master's: "I stand at the door and knock"⁷—*I*, the Christ, the son of God, *I* the presence of God, *I*, Immanuel, God with us, stands at the door of our consciousness and knocks.

In contemplating this passage, we discover why 9/10 of perhaps 99/100 of all prayers uttered to a God separate and apart from us are completely wasted and not answered. It is because, first of all, God is not outside us or above us, but actually within us knocking at the door of our consciousness, and the very first step that we must take is to admit God into our consciousness.

If we want to build a fulfilled life, a satisfactory year, a harmonious day, a successful business, and a happy family life, we will not succeed without the grace of God, without the realization of God's presence. The Master revealed the deep secret that the kingdom of God is within us, awaiting our acknowledgment, recognition, and invitation, but unless in this moment we acknowledge the truth of his revelation that the spirit of God is within us, how then can we take the next step and say, "Lord, I am listening. Enter."

Our very first task early in the morning, immediately upon awakening, is to turn within, acknowledge that *I*, the spirit of God, stands at the door of our consciousness and knocks, and then invite God to enter and take over our soul, mind, and body, take over the day, the household, the family, and the business. Having invited the presence of God to enter our consciousness, our attitude is one of receptivity to the Word.

Surrendering the Day to Omniscience and Omnipotence

Since the nature of God is omniscience, we need not tell God what things we need today, what amount, for whom, or for what. God is the all-knowing; and, therefore, it is enough to invite God to speak. The Master has revealed that He already knows our needs, so it is not necessary to talk to God, tell Him or ask Him for anything. We must follow the way the Master pointed out and accept the truth that God knows our need. God knows the need of this day, this hour, and this moment, and the presence of God fills that need. In His presence is fullness of joy, fullness of life, but only in His presence.

Where is the presence of God? Standing at the door of consciousness and knocking. But that is not enough until we have brought the presence of God consciously within and surrendered this day to that Omniscience which is omnipresent. We have invited the spirit of God within; and, since God is omnipotence, we have no problems to be overcome, no sins to be erased, no diseases to be healed, no fears to overcome. Omnipotence means all-power; therefore, there are no other powers.

> In My presence, there are no negative powers or
> evil powers. In My presence, "no weapon that is
> formed against thee shall prosper." [8] If you
> consciously admit Me into your soul, mind, and
> body, if you live and move and have your being in
> the consciousness of My presence within you,
> no evil can come nigh your dwelling place.

In God's presence is fullness, but if we do not begin our day with the presence of God, what right have we to expect fullness or fulfillment? "Where the spirit of the Lord is, there is liberty," [9] freedom. Where is this spirit of the Lord? Standing outside knocking at the door? Yes, until we, by invitation, say, "Enter and speak, Lord: Your servant is listening." Then the spirit of the Lord God is upon us, and we no longer live by might or by power, but by the grace of the spirit of God.

When we thus acknowledge the Presence within us, when we invite this Presence to take over our soul, mind, and body, business, home, and family, we are ready for the experience of actually witnessing that the spirit of God goes before us to "make the crooked places straight,"[10] to prepare "mansions"[11] for us. We find that we are living less and less by might and by power and more and more by divine Grace. This is an experience that only we can bring to ourselves.

The Experience of God Is Necessary

The Bible is full of spiritual truth, full of the word of God that can make of all our lives the dwelling place of God and reveal fulfillment. The Master points out the way when he says, "Ye shall know the truth."[12] He does not say that someone else shall know the truth for us. "Ye shall know the truth," and he proves by his ministry that the knowing of the truth by the grace of a spiritual teacher or practitioner can be a blessing to us in that some of our ills can be healed, some of our sins overcome, and some of our lacks removed. But this does not fulfill our life: this meets a temporary need. The fulfillment comes by an act of our own consciousness. It comes only by the invitation that flows through us and invites the spirit of God to enter.

"I and my Father are one."[13] But if I and the Father are one, how could you and I have had all the troubles we have known through these many years? The Infinite Way has revealed that the lost message was in the word "conscious" or "conscious awareness." All scripture reveals that it is only in our acceptance of God, our conscious realization of God, our actual experience of God that the presence of God is functioning within us.

The Spirit of the Lord is upon me,
because he hath anointed me to preach
the gospel to the poor; he hath sent me
to heal the brokenhearted, to preach
deliverance to the captives, and recovering of
sight to the blind, to set at liberty them
that are bruised.

Luke 4:18

Jesus was ordained to heal the sick only after the experience of receiving the spirit of the Lord God within him. So it is that we are ordained to live spiritually as children of God only when we have accepted and received His spirit within us and the spirit of God is upon us. To his disciples, he gave this same advice just before he ascended when he said, "Tarry ye in the city of Jerusalem until ye be endued from on high."[14] Without being endowed from on high, we are "man, whose breath is in his nostrils"[15]; we have no blessing to carry to the world; we have no spiritual benediction to utter; we have no healing grace to bestow; we have no words of comfort. These come only when the actual experience of Immanuel is ours, the actual experience of God with us.

The Reconciliation

This "natural man" of whom Paul spoke, "the creature," the man of earth, this is every one of us, and this is everyone who has ever lived, and this is everyone who will ever live in his sense of separation from God. It is only as, in one way or another, we are turned to a spiritual path that we begin to understand that we have been prodigals, living separate and apart from our spiritual inheritance, thinking ourselves to be something, and then, when we have been led this far, the way finally reveals itself to us as being the way of reconciliation.

We must reconcile ourselves to God and reconcile God to ourselves until there comes the actual relationship of oneness. Whereas there was God and man, through conscious reconciliation I and the Father are again realized as one and not two. Only then can we say that God is with us; or where God is, I am; and where I am, God is, for we are one. Dwelling in the conscious realization of that oneness, the reconciliation has taken place: God and man have become one, and that one is the one I am and the one you are.

Our years of search are merely years of reconciliation, reconciling ourselves to a life lived by the Spirit within us and as us. In a sense it is a life of surrender, because we are surrendering the universal belief of any personal sense of greatness and coming to understand life from the Master's standpoint of "If I bear witness of myself, my witness is not true,"[16] for "I can of mine own self do nothing,"[17] but then at another time, referring to that Spirit within which lived his life, he said, "I am the way, the truth, and the life."[18]

If we try to understand the Bible literally, we will believe that Jesus was declaring that he was the way, the truth, and the life, or that he was the resurrection, or that only he had meat that the world knew not of. To accept that is to be in the sad state of the world which is waiting for the second coming of the Christ and is suffering because of Its absence, in spite of the Master's being so clear on that point: "I will never leave thee, nor forsake thee."[19] There is no waiting for a second coming because *I* has never left us.

Our Good Unfolds from the I Within

This brings us to the word *I* as it is used in the New Testament. When the Master says, "I have meat to eat that ye know not of,"[20] we can be assured that he is saying that the presence of God in us is meat the world knows not of. "I am the resurrection and the life"[21] means that the *I* within us, the Christ of us, is the power of resurrection, not holy temples, not holy cities, not holy masters, but *I,* the spirit of God within us.

We can begin a whole new life based on the revelation that since the kingdom of God is within, our good must unfold from within. If we were composers of music, not copiers of somebody else's music, where would we go for the composition? Surely, not to the libraries to copy what somebody else had composed, but within our own consciousness where we have every right to expect something new, something heretofore unheard of to unfold. Why not? The nature of God is infinity. There must be an infinite number of melodies never yet heard by man, an infinite number of combinations of notes never before written down.

In the architecture of the new office buildings and residences, we are witnessing something entirely different from anything thought of thirty, forty, or fifty years ago. This was not copied from anywhere because it did not exist before now. Some of the great architects of this age have gone within, and they have found new forms of edifices to serve modern purposes. Some of these, many of us will agree, are not as beautiful as the older ones, according to our sense of beauty, but then we have no idea what the sense of beauty will be of those who are now growing up, and these buildings must satisfy their sense of beauty and not ours. Certainly they are more practical for the uses of today.

If we are going to build edifices of any nature—bridges, roads, airplanes, or forms of communication—the workers in those fields must learn to go within and draw forth through inspiration new ideas for this new age. Then we, too, will discover that all the spiritual wisdom that has ever existed on earth already exists within us. Furthermore, all the spiritual wisdom that has not yet been revealed to man exists within us awaiting our ability to turn within.

Whether we need ideas, whether we need finances to finance ideas, or whether we need materials, regardless of our needs, in this new spiritual age, we must learn that all that exists in the outer world has its substance within. Everything that is made is made from the substance of the Invisible, and all that exists within your consciousness and mine. The purpose of contemplation or meditation is the going within until, either through hearing the Word or feeling the Presence, we receive an inner assurance:

> *I* am on the field. My grace is with you.
> *I* have meat within you sufficient unto every
> need. *I* can give you living waters, and you
> will never thirst again. My peace give *I* unto you.

As we receive this assurance within, our demonstration is complete in the without, and we have only to be beholders and watch how fulfillment takes place.

No Alibis Are Permitted

We do not retire from the world to live in monasteries and convents, seaside cottages or mountaintop shacks: we remain in the world but not of it. We continue to do our daily work in the house with the family or do whatever our work may be, but with this difference: there is no worry about it, no fear, no anxiety, no concern, because the work of the outer plane is first being established on the inner level, and once it is established there, it has a way of fulfilling itself out here.

In our human experience as the man of earth, we have accepted the material sense of existence which says that, in order for us to fulfill our life, we are dependent on people, circumstances, conditions, or governments; and, therefore, every one of us has been provided with a wonderful alibi for failure. The government was not right; our parents were not right; our neighbors were not right; our employers were not right; our employees were not right; we did not have enough money. We all have perfect alibis so that we can rest peacefully in our failure, if we can be content with failure. But if we cannot be content with failure, then let us awaken to the fact that each one of us is an individual wholly dependent on the kingdom of God and Its grace that was established within us from the beginning.

Certainly, because of the spiritual ignorance of parents, grandparents, relatives, and friends, we have all known handicaps; we have all had difficult problems to meet; but while these may serve as alibis for those of the world, be assured they will not serve our purpose at all. To us has been revealed that great wisdom that the kingdom of God, the allness of God, is established within us "before Abraham was" and unto the end of the world. It has never left us or forsaken us, and never will.

Reconciliation As an Act of Consciousness

The Prodigal Son disinherited his father: the father never disinherited the son. When he turned to go back to the father's house, the father met him, and I am sure that it was more than halfway because that is the way it happens with us. When we turn to the realization that harmony, wholeness, completeness, fulfillment, liberty, freedom, joy, peace, and prosperity are not dependent on person, place, things, circumstances, or conditions external to us, but rather that they are dependent on our conscious union with our Source, we find that Grace within.

This reconciliation must be an act of consciousness. We have wandered so far from the Father's house that turning within for one day will not re-establish us. We must persist in daily meditation, daily contemplation of these scriptural truths and their spiritual significance, until we do understand that there is something within us so close that it was given the name *I*. It is

the presence of God, or son of God, the Christ of God, spiritual sonship. That is what this *I* is, and as we turn within in contemplation, it is that we may hear It say, " 'Son, thou art ever
with me, and all that I have is thine,'²² *I,* the spirit of God within you. All that *I* have is thine, Bill, Mary, William, or Robert,
son or daughter—all that *I* have, the *I* that is in the midst of
you, the *I* that has never left you, that will never forsake you."

The Power of I AM

We must raise up this *I,* the son of God, in all those we
meet, never forgetting our enemies, because to pray for our
friends profits us nothing at all. We must begin to look into
those countries, into those peoples, into those governments
where at the present time the Christ is not being shown forth
and recognize the son of God in the midst of them, recognize
that *I* in the midst of them.

When we recognize the Christ incarnate universally in man,
in saint and sinner, in the sick and the well, and in those we
erroneously call dead, we can take a very big step, probably one
of the biggest any of us has ever taken, and we can say, "There
is no power in heaven or on earth greater than *I AM.*" When
we say that, we will be saying that which will make it impossible for the weapons of the world to reach you and me or to
reach mankind, because we will be acknowledging the *I AM* in
the midst of them, and we will be acknowledging that there is
no outside power greater than the power of the *I* within them.
We will be raising up the son of God in saint and sinner, in the
walking dead, as well as those in the buried dead, neither or
which is really dead.

The living dead are those who eat and sleep and work separate and apart from their true identity, the ventriloquist's
dummy trying to live without the ventriloquist. The living are
those in whom the son of God has been lifted up and who know

that when they listen for the "still small voice,"[23] it will speak and it will say:

> *I* am in the midst of thee, and *I* in the midst of thee
> am mighty. *I* in the midst of thee am bread, meat,
> wine, and water. Because *I* am in the midst of thee,
> "no weapon that is formed against thee shall prosper."

> "Man, whose breath is in his nostrils," is hit by every
> weapon that has ever been conceived by man, but *I*,
> the son of God, in the midst of thee, am
> Omnipotence, Omnipresence, Omniscience. Nothing
> can prevail against that.

Only the conscious recognition of Omnipotence, Omniscience, Omnipresence as the "still small voice" within, only this sets us free from the weapons of this world: its mental weapons and its physical weapons.

The Role of Problems

Life could be very boring if it were just a repetition of all that went before. Every day brings forth new experiences and with them what the world calls problems. These must not be looked upon as if God had deserted us: they should be accepted as a part of everyone's normal routine existence, and we should recognize them as opportunities. Regardless of the name or the nature of the problems of daily experience, we realize the Presence, remembering that "He performeth the thing that is appointed for me to do."[24] This He that is referred to is that same *I* within us that is the spirit of God.

This passage of scripture has been greatly misunderstood and has been interpreted to mean that God performs whatever it is that we may wish, desire, or hope for. There is no scriptural authority for believing that God will perform that which pleases us. Before we can rest in the assurance that we have the spirit of God working with us and for us, let us first be sure that what is to be done is in accord with God's will, not necessarily our will.

Our Personal Will

There must be a period in the day in which we reconcile ourselves to God, surrender our desires or our will in the recognition of God's will and not ours. To be certain that we are not trying to live a life apart from the will of God, in our meditation we must return each day to the Father's house, to the Consciousness within, and ask for guidance, seeking only to do the will of God.

If, whether willfully or ignorantly, you and I stray from the will of God and let our human will take over, that will may not only not bless me, but probably will not bless you. Each of us has a responsibility, not only toward ourselves but toward the members of our family and our neighbors. We may think that we are an island alone, but no man can live as an island. We are all of the household of God, and therefore, each of us has an obligation, and that obligation is to love our neighbor as ourselves. The way to be certain that we are doing this is to be sure that we have surrendered our personal will and our personal desires that God may use us—soul, mind, and body—that our very presence may glorify God.

One way in which we show forth God's glory is to submit ourselves daily to His will, to His love, to His life, to His Spirit, and then let that "He" perform that which is appointed for us to do.

Let us give up the belief that we can lay out a plan for ourselves, made up of our desires, hopes, or will, and then ask God to prosper us. That would be making a servant of God. God does not perform our will. God does not undertake to prosper us in what we wish. God prospers us in that which God gives us to do. This becomes clearer to us if we think of God in terms of infinite spiritual consciousness, our individual consciousness. Then, as we learn to listen to that "still small voice" of our own consciousness, it reveals the divine will for us.

Life Is an Adventure

We must be careful that we are not too eager to settle down into a routine of whatever it is that we think of as Cloud Nine. We must not expect life to be just one round of sunshine every day because this could be as boring as the old idea of going to heaven and twanging a harp for eight hours a day and then sleeping the other sixteen hours.

From a spiritual standpoint, life is an adventure, and every day brings forth something new and different. This may not be true in the experience of the average person, because he usually wants only the dullness of the same routine every day, and very often is upset when that monotony is disturbed. This is not right for a person on the spiritual path because, not only is God infinite, but God is infinite in loving, God is infinite in imparting, God is infinite in grace; and, therefore, we can rightly expect an infinity of experiences: God-experiences, good experiences, but totally different one from the other and varying in nature. If every day we attuned ourselves to the way and the will of God, we would certainly be disappointed if we expected God to reveal Himself in the same way every day, because it will not be that way, nor will we always feel as if we were uplifted.

Vessels must be emptied in order to be filled, and in that emptying out process we may experience many days of barrenness, feeling that we are separated from God or that God for some reason has deserted us. God never deserts us: it is only that in the emptying out process we are deprived of that upon which we relied yesterday.

Here, too, in the metaphysical world especially, and very often in the spiritual world, we experience trouble. Some truth is revealed to us or given to us that does remarkable things for us, and then tomorrow we expect that same truth to do it over again, and it does not happen that way. The reason is that the power was not in the statement of truth that was given to us but in the consciousness from which it came. If we look to a statement of truth to do something for us, we will have built a golden calf, we will have expected spiritual power from an effect. A statement of truth is an effect. It is not truth, and it is not God. Our individual consciousness from which that statement came is God, and God fed us this meal with this truth, but then we are through with it. The next meal we will be fed differently with a different passage of truth or a different meaning to the same passage.

The passage "He performeth the thing which is appointed for me" was a very important one in my life. The part that I understood for many years was the first part: "He performeth." But very recently, I received a new light on that passage: that only that which God gives us to do does God perfect and perform. Whereas I had been fed for many years with the realization that there is a He within me that performs, now I was fed from an entirely different standpoint and enabled to change a whole attitude of life. In other words, now, more than ever, I could consciously surrender my soul, mind, and body every day to His will and His way.

The power of God is not in a Bible passage. The words are only the food, the substance with which God feeds us. God is our consciousness; therefore, the God-power is our consciousness. As we in meditation turn to it over and over again for every little item of the day, we are fed with the meat the world knows not of. We have all had the experience of receiving a passage of scripture and experiencing healing, uplift, or some spiritual blessing through it. Perhaps, too, we have had the experience of being disappointed at times when that same passage seemed to do nothing for us. By that time it had become "hash," and that was not our food for the moment.

The point is that we must be spiritually fed from God which is our individual consciousness. It is not always that we are fed with words or thoughts or quotations: sometimes we are fed just by a feeling of the Presence or an inner release of some kind, probably the release of mental or physical strain, something that attests to the presence of God realized. If we seek for statements of truth separate and apart from receiving them from consciousness, we seek amiss; we seek for power where it is not.

If we are reading the Bible and come to a specific passage which stands out, we may interpret this as our consciousness having given us that passage for the food immediately necessary, and then we may close the book and put it away, assimilating that food, digesting it, pondering it, and then going about our business. It is not the reading of the books that brings us to the kingdom of God; it is the assimilation of the passages that from time to time stand out, arrest our attention, and sometimes seem to be in electric lights.

The power is not in the Bible. If it were, the hundreds of millions of Bibles that are in this world would have saved the world. The power is not in the words that are in the Bible, or those words would have saved the world. The power is in the consciousness from which those words came, and if we read the Bible with that in mind, we will enter the consciousness of the mystics who wrote them, and from that consciousness will come forth our manna.

Across the Desk

Today I was led to pick up *Our Spiritual Resources,* perhaps because for some time this book has been out of print, but just recently we have received a shipment from England where it has now been republished.

In the first chapter, "A New Life by Grace," I found a treasure which is really the essence of all spiritual living. To grasp the principle set forth in that chapter is to live in the ever-presence of God's grace, operating and functioning now. It is not that anything we do makes this Grace operative in our experience, but that, as we surrender our will and desires and become inwardly still, we become aware of that Grace which is forever in operation. Any student who would live with that first chapter for a month or a year would find the new life by Grace his own experience.

Our Spiritual Resources is one of the most practical of all our Infinite Way writings. In fact, some students have said that if they could have only one Infinite Way book, that would be the one because it embodies the principles of spiritual living so clearly and concisely and in a way that leaves no doubt as to their practical application to everyday situations.

The following brief excerpt from it is the essence of the chapter and the book:

> Work, work, work, watch and pray—not for the purpose of influencing God, but for the purpose of purifying ourselves of any belief that God is a withholding, a punishing, or an avenging God. . . . Release God from any obligation to us and recognize that God's only obligation is to maintain and sustain His own spiritual universe. Set God free! God owes us nothing, but God owes Himself the joy of living freely and joyously—freely expressing, freely being—and we are the recipients of God's grace.
>
> God is forever in expression. And I shall live with the word *is*. God *is*, Good *is*, Life *is*, Infinity *is*, Omnipotence *is*, Omnipresence *is*. My prayer is to know this truth, not to set forces in motion.

Chapter Three

Let There Be Light

Far too often, we hear the statement, "Nothing is impossible to God." Usually those who voice that mean, "Well, then, we will just let God do all of this for us; and since nothing is impossible to God, we have nothing further to do." It is true that nothing is impossible to God, but that is not going to be of any help to you or to me except in proportion as we can bring the presence of God into actual realization. In other words, it is not the infinite, all-nature of God that makes our demonstration: it is the degree of our realization of that presence of God.

There was just as much of God in the world before the days of Jesus Christ; there was just as much of God in the world before the days of Moses. But what good did that do the Hebrews until there was a Moses to lead them out of their slavery? What good was all this infinite power of God until there was a Jesus to heal the sick, raise the dead, and feed the hungry? Spiritual healing was just as possible to the world throughout the past five thousand years as it is today, but of what avail was that to the world until Mrs. Eddy revealed that the presence of God is as available in this age as it was on the shores of Galilee?

It is true that God is and that God is infinite all-power and it is true that nothing is impossible to God; but only men like Moses, Elijah, Isaiah, Jesus, John, and Paul, who attained the actual realization and demonstration of God, were able to do these mighty works of spiritual regeneration, spiritual healing, and spiritual supplying.

This same condition exists today. Since the re-introduction of spiritual healing and spiritual living, there have been and there are now some of higher attained spiritual awareness than others, and thereby there are those who are doing greater works than others. The power of God is the same. The difference in demonstration is the difference in the degree of attained God-realization. Once we understand this, we will know that harmony in our individual life and in the life of our family or students is going to be in direct proportion to the degree of our attainment of spiritual awareness.

Spiritual Attainment, an Individual Responsibility

In more than thirty years, I have witnessed that there are many homes that have been kept wonderfully free of the discords of the world—not always completely without some problems coming in, but on the whole, beautifully free of the world's inharmonies—free because there is a mother in the family devoting herself to spiritual awareness; or in some homes, there may be even a mother and a father working together to this end. Where this is true, that household is comparatively untouched by the disasters, the destructions, and the discords of this world.

True, this statement cannot be one hundred percent demonstrated, for the simple reason that we have not attained one hundred percent of God-awareness; and, to some extent, the members of our household, just like the members of our student body, have a responsibility of their own. No one can wholly carry another into heaven. One member of a family can do wonders for the entire family, but he cannot maintain them all in complete freedom from discord for the simple reason that every individual has a responsibility for his own spiritual development, and no one can usurp that or take from him the privilege of going his materialistic way, if that is the way he wishes to go. We cannot take away from any person the individual expression of his own life, even when his life differs from the spiritual way. Therefore, no one should believe that he can guarantee complete immunity from discord to all the members of his household, because he cannot. But he certainly can be assured that the major disasters and destructions of life probably will not come nigh his household, and certainly in a great measure he can keep himself free.

An Understanding of Spiritual Principles
Is Important in Going Into Meditation

The measure of this freedom from world discords is in proportion to the degree of our attainment of God-realization, and meditation is the most important factor in attaining that realization, especially when that meditation is backed up with an understanding of the nature of spiritual principles.

If, however, we go into meditation with the idea that God is going to destroy sin, disease, lack, or limitation, we are setting up a barrier which prevents the very thing we are hoping for. So it is that in approaching meditation, we must realize that evil, regardless of its form, does not exist as a power in the realized presence of God; it does not exist as an entity or a force. Evil, whether it is in the form of sin, disease, lack, unemployment, wars, or threats of wars, exists only in the same way that darkness exists. Darkness is not an entity that goes somewhere when light is admitted to a room. Darkness is merely an absence of light. The moment light appears, there is no darkness; but darkness did not go any place; it has not moved out of the room. It was not in the room, there was not any "it"; there was merely an

absence of light. To perceive this is to understand the function
of meditation and spiritual healing.

Meditation Releases the Light Within

Meditation has for its purpose admitting the light which is
God, letting loose the light that is stored up within us. The kingdom of God, that is, spiritual light, is within us, and we must
open out a way for the light, hidden within, to escape.
Meditation, therefore, has nothing to do with overcoming sin,
disease, lack, or unemployment; it has nothing to do with stop-
ping evil men from continuing their evil practices. Meditation has
to do with us as individuals, realizing and releasing the light that
is within. In the attainment of that, the darkness disappears, and
the darkness is any and every form of human discord. The darkness and its forms vanish the very moment light is introduced.

We do not claim that we know how to heal disease, but we
do know how to sit and realize the impotent nature of anything
other than God's presence. "Thou couldest have no power at all
against me, except it were given thee from above."[1] There is no
power in darkness; there is no power in the forms in which
darkness appears: sin, disease, or lack. Therefore, we do not go
into meditation to overcome these; we do not go into meditation to destroy any of the evils of this world. We go into meditation that we may realize:

> I and the Father are one. Where I am, God is, and
> because of God's presence, there is peace, harmony,
> wholeness, and completeness. The place whereon I
> stand is holy ground, for in the presence of God
> there is the light of truth.
>
> God's presence is my sufficiency in all things. In
> God's presence is fulfillment, and I am here in medi-

tation to realize this truth and to be a transparency so
that the kingdom of God within me may be released
in consciousness, thereby dispelling every appearance
of darkness, every appearance of discord and inharmony. If I realize and feel the presence of God, everyone within range of my consciousness, receptive and
responsive to God, feels it, and feels the effects of it.

The Light Dissolves the Darkness

Every time that we attain, in meditation, an awareness, a
feeling, of God's presence, we have released the light into our
home, and then there are no dark places there any more: no
hidden errors, no sins, no diseases, no lacks. Where there is
light, darkness does not abide; where there is Spirit, there can be
no form of mortality. To realize God is to realize freedom and to
attain a complete release from fear.

> I have meat the world knows not of. I have
> within me the realization of a divine Presence,
> of a spiritual Light; and this is my bread, my
> meat, my wine, and my water. This is the law
> unto my life; this is the Presence that is
> within me always and goes before me.

We need not voice this; in fact, we must not voice it. "Pray
to thy Father which is in secret; and thy Father which seeth in
secret shall reward thee openly."[2] In secret, we realize God's
grace and His presence; in secret, we realize the spiritual nature
of the function of God. In proportion as we feel an inner
release, an inner confidence, we can be assured that we have
attained some measure of spiritual light; and then we go about
our daily tasks, whatever their name or nature may be, and leave
the rest to that realized presence of God.

We have been told by the Master to be in the world, but not of it. This means that unless we sit down for a meditation several times during the day, we will soon find that we are again embroiled in "this world"—its fears and its discords.

Recently, something came to my attention that bore witness to the evil nature of some of the men in positions of power who are manipulating the world, and for a moment it brought a sense of inner disturbance. But almost simultaneously the Voice spoke and said, "But there are not any evil men: man is spiritual." That brought a complete release from being in and of the world, or of being under the influence of its fears and worries. Did that realization remove these evil men from the world? No, it removed them and any effect they might have from my consciousness as well as from the consciousness of those who are attuned to my consciousness.

Our Function Is the Realization of the Presence, Not Overcoming Problems

We can be responsible only for our own state of consciousness. We need not ask the members of our family to believe in spiritual healing or spiritual living; we need not try to convince them of the benefits they could receive from it. It is far better to accept responsibility for our own state of consciousness and leave the other members of our household to work out their unfoldment, and if they are to be brought to our way of life, they will come rather by our example than by our preaching.

This does not, however, extend to the children of our household, because we have accepted the responsibility for the care of the children who have been given to us, for their instruction and their guidance until they reach the age when they may go off and live their own life. Usually they will go off and live in accordance with what they have received in their homes.

Our purpose in our morning meditation and in the other

meditations during the day or night is always the realization of God's presence, always remembering that we do not have problems to overcome, that we have only to attain the realization of God's presence, and It, by being the light, will dispel the darkness, not dispel it by overcoming it or destroying it, but by proving that in the presence of light, there is no darkness. Thereby, we shall prove that in the presence of God, there is fulfillment. In the presence of God, there is no sin, no disease, no lack, no unemployment, no war; and if we were at the very front of the battle, there would still be no war for us in the presence of God realized.

Our First Consideration Is the Development of Our Own Consciousness

The reason for the study of the writings, for hearing the tape recordings, and for attending Infinite Way classes is the deeper and richer attainment of God-awareness. If we understand this, we will have an easier approach to our daily living, because once we perceive this point, we will know why we meditate. We will know why, before engaging in the world's activities, it is important to begin our day with a period of meditation for the purpose of the attainment of spiritual realization.

Our only responsibility at this stage of our unfoldment is the development of our own spiritual consciousness. At first, it may seem a bit selfish to leave the rest of the world alone and concern ourselves only with that; but ultimately we will find that this particular form of selfishness is the height of unselfishness, because once we attain some measure of God-realization, then the world will beat a pathway to our door and really be benefitted by the degree of consciousness that we have attained.

No one can be benefitted spiritually by going to anyone who is merely a human being: a person can be benefitted only by going to a degree of attained spiritual realization. Therefore, it is the height of unselfishness to let the world alone temporarily, while we study, meditate, and attain a measure of Christ-realization. After that, every time a call is made upon us, we answer it and fulfill ourselves. Then there is no fear that we do not yet understand enough or that we have not enough spiritual power, because there never will come a time when we understand enough, and there never will come a time when we have spiritual power. All that we can do in our most advanced state is what we can do in our beginning state, and that is, let the light dispel the darkness. "Let there be light: and there was light"[3]—let there be God, God functioning and His presence going before us.

Accept Every Problem As a Call to Recognize the Light Within

When we observe discords and inharmonies in our home, this is an opportunity to begin our practice, and that practice consists of meditating until we feel the presence of God, and then let it perform its function. Eventually, as the light dawns more and more in our consciousness, we will find that others will come to us. At first, it will be a miracle how they even knew that we were interested in spiritual things. It is always puzzling as to how people discern this without even knowing; but as they come, we do not send them away: we accept the responsibility, taking this attitude: "If God sent this individual to me, then it is only that God may respond, and so I will meditate." Our whole responsibility is to feel that inner assurance of God's presence, and let it perform the work.

We are not responsible for saving anybody's life; we are not responsible for healing anybody for we do not have this capacity, nor does anyone else; but we do have the responsibility for being in this world, but not of it. We do have the responsibility of retiring several times a day for meditation, for the realization of God's grace as our sufficiency, of God's presence as the light which dispels the darkness, and then abiding in our meditation until we feel this Presence.

We are not trying to reform people; we are not trying to heal people; we are not trying to change the conditions of this world: we are sitting in meditation to attain the realization of God's grace and God's presence. That is our only purpose, and in proportion as we succeed, we will witness how the darkness evaporates out of our life, out of our household, out of the experience of the members of our household, and then gradually, how this darkness is dispelled in the experience of those who come to us.

Release Man and Release God

But let us not be tempted to go back to the erroneous practice of believing in a mental cause for disease. Evil does not have its existence in the consciousness of any individual. Nobody causes his own problems, except through ignorance of truth. Every problem that we have in our experience is the degree of our ignorance of truth. Evil has a universal source: the carnal mind, human consciousness, or any name you want to give it; but it is absolutely impersonal.

A basic principle of the Infinite Way is that evil does not have its rise in us, nor does evil have its rise in God. The religious teaching that God is responsible for acts of evil, for the diseases or the death of human beings, that God calls human beings home, is no part of our teaching because the direct revelation has been given to us in the Infinite Way that no evil has its rise in God. God is not responsible for any of the evils that have befallen mankind. Neither does evil have its rise in individual you or me. All evil has its source in the universal belief in two powers, in the universal belief that we are a selfhood apart from God, in the universal belief that there are laws other than the spiritual laws of God.

Evil, a Belief in Two Powers

In the degree, then, that we begin to purge ourselves of the belief that any of the evils in human experience emanate from God, we can go a step further and realize that the discords of life do not have their rise in us, but that evil of any form or nature—even tidal waves or winter storms—has its rise in the carnal mind, which is merely a belief in two powers. Without this belief, nothing could ever be destructive, nothing could ever be harmful, nothing could ever be painful. So we have as the basic source of all evil the universal belief in two powers, constituting the mesmeric suggestion, mesmeric mind, or mesmeric belief that in the end manifests itself in our bodies, in our business, and in our affairs.

We turn in meditation, and realize that evil does not have its source in God, nor does evil have its source in man. Evil, the darkness, is really made up of a belief in two powers, and this belief has no law of God to sustain it; it has no divine authority; therefore, it is without form and void. Then turn within:

> "Speak Lord; for thy servant heareth."[4] When Thou
> utterest Thy voice, the earth melteth. Therefore, in
> this meditation, I am a transparency that Thy will
> may be done on earth as it is in heaven.

We have just acknowledged that God's will does not include acts of destruction, sin, disease, or death. If we really want to know what God's will is, let us read the gospels and see why Jesus came to earth, what his mission was, and the source of his mission, and we shall find that the will of God is that we be healed, that we be enriched, that we be fed, that we be raised from the dead, that we be enlightened. That is why he came to earth; that is why he gave this message: "I am come that they might have life, and that they might have it more abundantly."[5]

And this is the will of God. Therefore, when we pray, "Thy will be done in earth, as it is in heaven,"[6] we really are praying that health, wholeness, harmony, peace, abundance—all of these—be made manifest on earth, as they are in the spiritual reality of the kingdom of God within us.

Attain the Center Within
That the World May Know Peace

There is a center within each one of us in which is complete harmony, complete spiritual rest and peace, a complete sabbath from this world. There is that center within each of us, and eventually in our meditation we reach it and actually sit in that center within our own being in an eternal peace, a divine state of peace. The storms of this world do not enter there. In that state of inner peace, we pray that this eternal peace at the center of our being—this eternal harmony, wholeness, completeness, and perfection—now may be made manifest on earth as it is within us. If we have within us this center of divine peace, rest, and sabbath, and we meditate, it is only that we may be still and let this glory escape, so that all men may feel the divine presence and power that is at the center of our being and which we have realized.

This, in turn, reveals that since it is true "that God is no respecter of persons,"[7] this same divine center is at the center of all being, and everyone receptive to the spiritual impulse can retire from the world in meditation, be separate and apart from the world, be in the world, but not of it, and finally realize that he, too, has "meat"[8] that the world knows not of. He, too, has this center where peace is enshrined. He, too, has this inner center of light, and therefore it is possible for him to open out a way for that imprisoned light to escape. As he does, he may be assured that the storms out here will begin to subside. They may at first be only the storms that are in his own mind and body;

later they will be the storms that are in his household and in the members of his family; and then later he will draw to him those to whom he can give this same Light.

"Ten" Righteous Men

Do you believe that "ten"[9] righteous men in a city could save the city? I hope you really believe that. I hope you believe that one hundred persons in this world could save the world from all the disasters that threaten it. Just one hundred persons, or even less, could do that. One individual like Moses influenced and benefitted the entire Hebrew race of his day. One man like Jesus Christ brought benefits untold to millions of people for twenty centuries, and probably his work will benefit more from now on than even up to this present time. Think how the life of Mrs. Eddy has affected the entire religious world throughout the globe and how many millions of people have experienced physical, mental, moral, and financial healings through that one woman's consciousness. If you stop to think of that, then you must realize the power there is in the spiritual consciousness of one individual.

For brevity's sake, I mention only a few, but there are so many others whom you could name who have influenced and blessed the lives of numberless persons and brought peace and harmony. As you read about the lives of the religious lights of the world and see the influence that every individual one of them has had on countless thousands, and sometimes millions, you will understand what I mean when I say that "ten" righteous men and women could save the entire world.

But what do we mean by righteous? What do we mean by "ten" righteous men? It has nothing to do with people of good morals; it has nothing to do with people who rigidly follow some religious teaching. The word "righteous" has to do with attained spiritual consciousness; it has to do with a developed spiritual awareness, the same mind "which was also in Christ Jesus,"[10] the same consciousness that has influenced all spiritual lights.

The Spirit that animated Lao-tse and Buddha is the very same Spirit that animated Jesus Christ; and the Spirit that animated Jesus Christ is the self-same Spirit that has animated every spiritual light, male or female, throughout all time. In other words, there is only one Spirit, and there is only one spiritual consciousness, and the Spirit that performed Its work through Moses, Elijah, Elisha, Isaiah, Jesus, John, and Paul, that same Spirit is the Spirit of every individual who attains spiritual consciousness. In other words, they attained the consciousness of the Spirit that has animated every spiritual light; therefore, It has the same power; It has the same influence; and It always does the same miraculous work.

Receptivity and Healing

None of us should be discouraged if we cannot benefit all whom we would like to benefit, because we must remember that there must be some degree of spiritual receptivity and responsiveness in those to whom we give help. Usually the mere fact that they will ask for help indicates that they have that degree of spiritual receptivity. Many persons ask us to take up work for Jones, Brown, or Smith somewhere, someone who is not interested in spiritual truth and is in a hospital or is receiving medical aid. They say that he deserves to be well because he is a loving father or has some other good human quality, as if we could go around entering the household of anybody and everybody who is sick. We cannot, but surely we can bring some measure of light to everyone open, receptive, and responsive to it. That is our responsibility.

Eventually, by this light, we shall find that more and more in the world are receptive to It, and that is why we have every reason to believe and to hope that we are rapidly approaching the age of harmony in world affairs. Let us not be any more discouraged by the day-to-day news than we may be when doing healing work for the sick and finding that for a while they get worse or that they do not improve. That is no cause for discouragement, as long as we are faithfully doing the work that is ours and our patient or student is faithfully doing his, because all healing work does not evolve in the same way. Very often healings do not take place until some specific truth has been realized, or some specific discord or other has to be removed from our consciousness before the harmony can appear in the body. In other words, we are never to judge by appearances.

All we are responsible for is the depth of our meditation, our attainment of God-realization, and then the government is on Its shoulder to perform Its work in Its way. Our responsibility goes only as far as bringing about an immediate release; the responsibility of the person asking for help lies in attaining the higher consciousness that will prevent this problem from recurring.

Within Us Is the Light of the World

Whenever we come together in any or every phase of our work, let us realize that deep at the center of our being there is this enthroned Christ, the Light of the world. Regardless of what words might be spoken, there would be no particular benefit unless at the same time there was an actual realized presence of God. In other words, the mere form of the message that comes through is not the important part of any meeting: the importance will be the degree of realized Christ, of realized God, and this must take place within our consciousness.

The reason that we come together is to experience God; and we should never meet except for that specific purpose. "Where the Spirit of the Lord is, there is liberty,"[11] and anything less than the actual presence of God will not serve our particular purpose.

Within me and within you is this Light of the world, that which can save the world. The Saviour of mankind is enthroned within us, and we are going into meditation for the purpose of being still, and realizing the "meat" the world knows not of. In the meditation, this Light, this "meat," is to be released and go out into human consciousness as light dispelling the darkness. Even though we do not humanly voice this truth, even though we sit in silence, the very walls will emanate light, give light and comfort and healing.

Across the Desk

Have you ever sat down with a concordance to the Bible and looked up the references on light? If you have not done so, you have a surprise and a treat ahead of you, because not only our Bible but the scriptures of the world abound in references to light as symbolical of spiritual attainment, climaxing in that illumination in which the whole world becomes new.

Each one of you who engages in this type of spiritual study will find his own special passages by which to live, and most certainly new unfoldments will be revealed to those who pursue this subject of spiritual light and contemplate its nature. Then, in his heart, the call will come to "Arise, shine; for thy light is come, and the glory of the Lord is risen upon thee . . . . And the Lord shall be unto thee an everlasting light, and thy God thy glory."

What a wonderful month of deepened consciousness this could be if every student who reads this *Letter* would use light as a subject of study and meditation! That Light would become such an activity of consciousness that the shadows of world belief and suggestion would fade away in the presence of its glory.

Tape Recorded Excerpts
Prepared by the Editor

The spiritual path is a journey from darkness to light, an emergence out of the density and grossness of human consciousness into the light of spiritual realization in which there is no darkness. When this light comes, a light that is not a physical light, but the enlightenment of consciousness, consciousness is then said to be illumined. Many of the Infinite Way tape recordings deal with the subject of illumination and give practical hints about what it is, of ways of attaining that illumination, and the signs and fruitage of it. The following excerpts are nuggets culled from a number of such tape recordings.

Illumination

"In the Oriental countries, those who were interested in attaining spiritual illumination, spiritual light, went to a teacher and, as a rule, lived with or near the teacher over a period of six, seven, or eight years, and by means of meditation with and without the teacher, meditation with other students and certain studies, they eventually attained their illumination. . . .

"The question is not one of attaining at first that degree of illumination which would set us up as spiritual teachers or spiritual healers, but how to attain sufficient illumination or enlightenment to be able to free ourselves from the discords, the inharmonies of human living, and build up within ourselves a spiritual sense that would not only lift us above the world's troubles, family troubles, or community troubles, but would enable us to live our normal human family, business, or professional life, and yet be inspired, fed, supported by an inner experience, an inner contact.

"Illumination can never come to a person who is seeking it: it can come only to those who realize that the kingdom of God—of Light, of Truth, of Wisdom, of Love—is within. . . . The entire secret of spiritual illumination is bound up in that realization that the kingdom of God is within, and I must find a way to let this 'imprisoned splendor' escape.

"The first step is always our consciously knowing the

truth, intellectually knowing the truth, and then, through this constant pondering, meditation, and cogitating, we bring ourselves to the place where we've said it all and thought it all, and now are still. Then into that stillness and up from that stillness comes the very light that we have been seeking."

Joel S. Goldsmith. "Starting the Contemplative Life,"
The 1960 Maui Open Class. Reel 3, Side 1.

"When you are at the stage where Something greater than yourself is pushing you into a spiritual path, then it is that you can choose. You have the opportunity to determine how many hours a day you will give to it or what degree of effort you will make to attain the stillness and silence of meditation. You can determine whether or not you will set aside periods to practice the letter of truth until it becomes the spirit of truth. It rests within your power to determine whether your ultimate illumination or realization will come in one year, three, five, or whether it will be drawn out into twenty. . . .

"Of this you may be sure: your ultimate realization and illumination are already assured. The finger of God is upon you, or you would not be following any spiritual path. You would be satisfied to demonstrate loaves and fishes. . . . But once you have gone beyond the place where immediate demonstration is the first consideration to where you realize that if you never demonstrated your health or your supply, you nevertheless could not turn back from the spiritual path. . . the rest is inevitable. . . . But no man can tell what minute the spark of illumination will rise in you."

Joel S. Goldsmith. "From the Law,"
The 1960 Chicago Closed Class, Reel 1, Side 1.

"Spiritual illumination consists of knowing God aright, and you will never know God aright while you give God a name, an identity, or a form. . . . Do not make anything at all to symbolize God, because in your mind, you must keep yourself absolutely free of any concept; and when you have no concept at all, you will find that God has become your life, your being, your health, your supply. . . .

"When your mind is unconditioned, you are standing in the very presence of God. That means when you have no finite concepts, when you are willing to erase from your mind whatever it is that you believed about God, whatever you believed about spiritual creation, or whatever you believed about anything else. Erase it all from your mind and be taught of God because. . . you can turn within at any time for enlightenment on any subject."

Joel S. Goldsmith. "Illumination: Its Nature,"
The Second 1960 London Closed Class. Reel 3,Side 1.

"The goal of our work is spiritual living or the attainment of spiritual consciousness in some degree. This may also be called illumination. What it really means is that since human beings are people entirely cut off from God—not under the law of God, not supported or maintained or sustained by God, nor protected—the object of human life must inevitably be to return to the Father's house, to attain some measure of spiritual light which will result in again becoming children of God. . . . This process was called illumination. Those who were illumined were those who had risen above mortal or material consciousness, those who had received light and in some cases initiation."

Joel S. Goldsmith. "Immanuel, Omnipresence, Omnipotence,"
The 1960 England Open Class. Reel 2, Side 1.

Chapter Four

Easter: An Experience
of Consciousness

To think of Easter as commemorating the resurrection of a man who died or was crucified two thousand years ago is not experiencing the real meaning of Easter; it is not being conscious of its great significance. Resurrection is an experience. It is an experience of truth, and the purpose of the Master's resurrection was not merely to prove that he could raise himself up from the dead, because of what value would that be to us? No, it was to exemplify his basic teaching that the dead are to be raised, whether "dead" in sin, "dead" in lack, "dead" in ignorance, or "dead" in disease. The dead are to be resurrected, raised up into life again.

As a matter of fact, the idea of resurrection is a part of the teaching of all mysticism, all religious teachings, and all truth-teachings. There are persons who are sick, sinning, dying, and dead, and without resurrection, that is where they remain. There are persons in the prison of their mentality, and without resurrection, that is where they are left. Eventually, all mankind must be resurrected, must be raised out of the inertia of humanhood which in itself is death. Simply continuing on and on in the same old pattern, this is inertia, this is "death."

The Master proved that to be resurrected took something

more than having twelve disciples around him, or eleven, and asking them to pray with him. There is more to resurrection than that. Probably many of those disciples were very good practitioners or healers, and although Jesus did ask them to stay awake and to pray with him, this did not result in his resurrection. In the end, he had to pray alone; in the end, he had to realize his own resurrection and ascension. Why was that? To understand the reason, we must begin with the premise that the crucifixion, resurrection, and ascension took place within his own consciousness.

It is true that part of our resurrection comes because of the Master's experience and the experience of his disciples. Our resurrection, in a measure, comes because we have found spiritual teachers or practitioners to help us on the way, but be assured that these are only temporary helps. Our resurrection comes through an activity of our own consciousness. Something must take place within us that ultimately leads to the Easter Day, that is, the actual experience of resurrection.

Resurrection, an Activity of Consciousness

Whatever happens to anyone must happen as an experience of consciousness. Without an activity of my individual consciousness, nothing can happen to me, for good or for evil. Without an activity of your individual consciousness, nothing can happen to you. We live only in proportion to the conscious activity of our being. Otherwise we are not conscious. So many persons are nothing but the walking dead—unconscious: dead emotionally, intellectually, and spiritually. No one is alive unless something is taking place in his consciousness, something of which he is consciously aware.

What the Master did during his early years and what he did during his three years of ministry culminated in whatever took place in his consciousness in Gethsemane, and on that final walk to Golgotha. All those experiences added together must have come to a focus in those last twenty-four hours and enabled him to make the final demonstration on earth of resurrection, and probably paved the way for the next realization, which resulted in the ascension. Resurrection is not something that happened to the Master from outside, nor is ascension something that happened to the Master from outside. Resurrection and ascension were actual activities of the consciousness of the Master, and without this activity, whatever its nature, there would have been no resurrection and there would have been no ascension.

The Struggle Is Always Within Ourselves

In my many years in this work I have discovered that whatever harmony, grace, beauty, or prosperity, whatever measure of success, love, health, or joy has come into my experience has come through the years of struggling inside with myself, aided by books, teachings, and teachers, but ultimately through a struggle within my own consciousness to attain something.

In the beginning, I had only one goal, and that was to discover why God is not in the human universe, why God does not stop wars or prevent them, why God does not stop or prevent murders, rape, arson, and suicides. Why is God not in this human picture? To find the answer to that question was my goal, and the struggle lasted exactly twenty years, from 1909 to 1929, until the first answer came. The struggle could have taken place only in my consciousness because I had no knowledge then, as I have no knowledge now, of any other place to find the answer to that particular question.

Is There a Response Within You to This Message?

Since then I have discovered that some of our students attain glorious experiences in life, beautiful harmony and peace, and the most satisfying and joyous contacts with the Father within. With each and every one of them, I know that regardless of what help I may have been to them and regardless of what help these writings may have been, their success did not come through me or through the writings: their success came through the struggle that took place in their consciousness to embody that which is in this message. The message itself will not do it.

I have known many persons who have read these writings and then given them away, even sold them to second-hand book stores, because they thought that there was nothing in them. There was nothing in them for them because there was no receptivity in their consciousness to do something with what they read in the writings. What is in them alone will not do it: it is what a person's individual consciousness does with what is in the message that does it.

From now until doomsday, we can repeat that God is good, God is love, God cares for His own. We can even go a step further, along with all our metaphysical friends, and say that evil is not power, sin is not power, or disease is not power, and all the while we can be sick, sinning, poor, dying, and dead, because until there is an answering response within our own consciousness, this message remains only the letter of truth that "killeth." Paul was very clear on that: "For the letter killeth, but the spirit giveth life."[1] At least if it does not kill, it does not cure.

The letter of truth does not cure, and although reading Infinite Way books sometimes results in individual healings, that is not the object of our work. The real cure is when the resurrection and the ascension take place, when we are raised up out of mortality into immortality, when we ascend above humanhood into our Christhood. This was the object of the Master's message. That is why he spoke so sadly about those who came to him only for the loaves and fishes. "Verily, verily, I say unto you, Ye seek me, not because ye saw the miracles, but because ye did eat of the loaves, and were filled."[2] Whether the "loaves and fishes" meant food or healing, it made no difference. Those who came only for loaves and fishes missed the entire message of the Master. So it was that after he fed them and they came back the next day for more, he rebuked them.

To live a spiritual message inevitably results in the added things, but these added things are not the goal. The goal is resurrection and ascension; the goal is putting off mortality and putting on immortality: the goal is "dying" daily to our humanhood and being spiritually reborn into our Christ-Self, the reality of us. But this must be understood to be an activity of consciousness, and insofar as it is to affect you or me, it is an activity of your consciousness and of my consciousness.

What the Master Proved

As human beings, we can wait for Easter Day to come around on the calendar, and celebrate this special day with Easter eggs, turkey, ham, and other things, even pausing briefly to remember that two thousand years ago Jesus was raised from the tomb. There will be millions of others doing that very same thing, but what value that is to them I do not know, nor do I know what they gain from it.

From the experience of Jesus, I understand that he meant to prove that what he accomplished, we can accomplish by following in the way he taught, by following the way he lived. He was the Exemplar; he was the Wayshower; he set forth the truth that we can attain immortality. We can attain a resurrection from the tomb; we can be set free from the prison of our minds, the prison of sin, of false appetite, of disease, or the prison of old age, because we should never forget that none of these things actually exists anywhere except in the mind of man.

Re-identification

In reality, there is no such thing as old age. Age does exist, however, as a universal belief in the mind of man, a belief which we individually accept. So, as long as we entertain in thought the belief that each passing day or each passing year makes us older, that is what we shall demonstrate. We cannot be resurrected out of the belief of age until we re-identify ourselves.

The Master set forth the manner of re-identification when he said, "Destroy this temple, and in three days I will raise it up."[3] Here he declared the immortality of his individual being, because he was saying that even if this temple, this body, were destroyed *I* would still be there to raise it up. Later he proved this when those who crucified him attempted to destroy the body. They made very sure that he was dead. But he was not! That *I* of which he spoke with such confidence was omnipresent, omniscient, omnipotent, and therefore *I* was right there to perform the miracle of resurrection, raising the body from the tomb.

Raising Up the Temple of God

So it is with you and with me. We also have a temple which we have thought of as a human body, which it is not. Actually it is the temple of God, the body of God. Only our false concept of the body makes it appear to us as a human body, but this body really is the temple of God. Just as your body is given to you for your use, so is mine given to me as a vehicle, as an instrument, for my use, for as long as I shall need it on earth. There will be a right time to drop this body, a time when no further service can be performed on earth, a time when my mission is completed, a time when my work is done and my obligations have been fulfilled. Then the time will come to drop this sense of body and go on. But I will not drop *Me: I* will live forever.

Should some experience of the race-mind threaten my body before my work is finished, then, according to the Master's revelation, since *I* am still here, *I* can raise up and resurrect this body from disease, even from death itself, if it should strike. *I* can do this, because *I* will never leave me nor forsake me, *I* am with me always. *I* am eternally alive, and *I* will be alive eternally. At least as long as God lives, *I* will live, for the life of God and the life of me are the same life. There is only one life, and my life is as eternal as God. Therefore, if this temple is destroyed before I am ready to give it up, *I* will raise it up again. *I* will raise it out of disease; *I* will raise it out of any sin, any temptation, or any false appetite. *I* will raise it out of lack or limitation, because *I* am always here where I am. If I mount up to heaven, *I* am here, "if I make my bed in hell,"[4] *I* am here, if I "walk through the valley of the shadow of death," [5] *I* am here, for "I and my Father are one."[6] The life of God and my life are one.

Establishing Truth in Consciousness

This cannot be accomplished by reading about it in books. That is the letter of truth. There must first of all be something in me, in you—in us—that responds to the Message and says, "Ah, yes! This is truth!" Then we must abide in that Word and let that Word abide in us. We must live with this truth over and over again.

> *I* am the life of this body; *I* am the law unto this
> body; and *I* am come that this body might have life
> and that it might have life more abundantly.
> *I* am come that my experience might be fruitful.
> *I* have "meat" [7] the world knows not of; *I* have
> "hidden manna." [8]

But we must live with the truth of scripture; we must let that truth abide in our consciousness. We must abide in that Word. We must sing the same song from morning to night, and certainly it must be our very last thought before sleeping, so that we carry it into our sleep with us, because we must not lose consciousness even when we are sleeping. We must be conscious twenty-four hours a day, even when we are at rest. Our consciousness must be alive with this truth:

> "I and my Father are one," and all that the Father has
> is mine. I have a "hidden manna" which is life eter-
> nal. "I am the bread of life" [9]—*I* embody the bread of
> life. If, for any reason, this body is destroyed,
> *I* will raise it up. *I* will be there; Consciousness will
> be right there to revive it, to heal it, to renew it, as
> long as *I* have any earthly use for it.

But this must be an activity of our consciousness.

Consciousness Is Not Limited to a Body

I have had the experience of being taken into my Master's household, into my Master's consciousness, into my Master's temple, even the cave where my Master lives, *the* Master, for there is but one. This is an experience of consciousness in which the body travels just as rapidly as thought. You can make this an activity of your consciousness by closing your eyes now for a moment and thinking about the home where you live. If you have lived in Hawaii, look outside on the street and immediately move to the shore at Waikiki. Go right out on the sand in front of the Royal Hawaiian, the Halekulani, or Kuhio Beach—any place along Waikiki. See how rapidly we have moved there, not only mind, but body as well—not corporeality, but body. We did not leave the body to go there: we have our body right while we are standing on the beach. So, if we like, we can move right up to the top of the Pali and look out on that valley, and instantaneously we are there, and we are there in our same body and same form.

This is not an experience of imagination: this is an experience of consciousness. It happens that we find this very easy to do, because we have gone only to the places with which we are familiar. But remember that just as we can move about so readily in the places with which we are familiar, so with an activity of consciousness we could move about just as freely to any part of this globe, even into the other planets, into the skies, and down beneath the waters, because everything that takes place in our consciousness must take place as an activity of our consciousness. Not even our body can move without an activity of our consciousness moving it.

Being an Individual

The life of the human vegetable, the so-called walking dead, is usually a life lived without conscious awareness, and life moves in on them and moves them around, here, there, and the other place. From their point of view, all the good things that happen are due to themselves, but all the bad things that happen are always due to somebody else, to somebody else's evils, or to some other experience. But it is not so. Persons permit themselves to be acted upon; they do not live their own life; they do not take their life into their consciousness and govern it: they let themselves be acted upon. If the world says that people catch cold by sitting in a draft or getting wet feet, so be it unto them, and so it happens to them. When medical authorities decide that people cannot catch cold merely by sitting in a draft, then they do not catch cold that way any more. None of this is of their own doing; all of this is because they are being acted upon by the forces of human belief.

We can be individuals only by an activity of our own consciousness, determining for ourselves the nature of the thoughts that we are to think, and not accepting everything that appears in print, even those things that are in print because someone believes them to be good and true. Each one of us has this same infinite consciousness, and each one can evaluate what goes into his mind. Of course in the doing of it, we may make many mistakes, but we have no right to be afraid of mistakes. Sometimes these mistakes lead us to the right path.

One reason that most of us are living in countries where there is freedom to express is because in such countries we are, if we would like to be, permitted to be individuals. There is no one telling us how to think, when to think, or what to think about. If we wish to exercise the privilege, we can be individuals.

Only the Grace of God Makes Possible a Life of Conscious Awareness

The important thing is that at some time or other we determine that we will be resurrected and that we will ascend. Without this conviction and determination, of course, the years will just pass by, and we will continue to be acted upon by every wind that blows. But in a given moment, when we can accept the truth that the resurrection of Christ Jesus was a lesson—not a talk and not a lecture—then we can begin the process of consciously abiding in the Word, consciously letting the Word abide in us until, in a moment that we think not, all of a sudden it happens: "the Son of man cometh,"[10] the actual experience of resurrection comes and eventually that of ascension.

Of ourselves, we cannot choose to do this. This I say to you most regretfully; this I say to you very sadly, after having witnessed for more than thirty years that it is so. Of our own accord, we cannot even determine to live consciously, we cannot determine to abide in the Word and let the Word abide in us.

We cannot do this. It is only by the grace of God, it is only when we have been touched that something within us responds and we say, "I can begin," or, "I am going to begin," or, "This is my path."

Each one in turn waits for that time when the spirit of God touches him and awakens him to the possibilities of the spiritual life. Even then it is given to us to begin only slowly. We can begin probably by reading or hearing truth, thirty, forty, or sixty minutes in a day. More than that, it is very difficult to take at first. Eventually, as we persist, it becomes two hours, and three, and ultimately we reach the goal: "Pray without ceasing"[11]; know the truth without ceasing; abide in the Word without ceasing; day and night live consciously in it always; and never live, not even for a moment in the day, in such a way as to permit the human mind to have its way with us.

Becoming a Law Unto Oneself

A few years ago there was an attempt to bring subliminal perception into advertising. It was a system by which thoughts were projected into individual consciousness. A person did not hear it and did not see it, but all of a sudden he jumped up out of his seat and felt that he must have a bag of peanuts or a bottle of Coca-Cola. This actually happened in experiments. Nobody knew why he had this sudden urge: he just had to do it.

All human beings have the urge to do things and think things which they know are not good for them, and when they cannot control that desire, they become victims of it. This is because we have lived for centuries letting the universal beliefs of the world influence us and have power and jurisdiction over us. We have lived so as to let ignorance and superstition and fear govern us, whereas none of this is necessary. It is not necessary to be victims of ignorance, superstition, and fear.

There is a secret that was known to the ancients and was

taught by the Master, even though the manuscripts that are available to us do not indicate how he taught it, and that is that we can be a law unto ourselves by abiding in the Word and letting the Word abide in us, by living, moving, and having our being in God-consciousness instead of man-consciousness, by living and dwelling "in the secret place of the most High,"[12] instead of dwelling in carnal thoughts, carnal hopes, and carnal ambitions.

The Inner Drive to God-Realization

At some moment of our lives, when we are prepared to accept it, truth is presented to us, and from that moment on, we have no choice. We must accept it, even though at first with hesitation, even though at first we take it, drop it, pick it up again, and drop it again, and even though at first it may be for one hour a week or one hour a day. Regardless of how halting or slow the beginnings may be, It, the spirit of God within us, will not let us alone, and It will keep nagging and plaguing us until eventually the light dawns.

This was the experience of Saul of Tarsus. When he voluntarily gave up his free citizenship to live among the Hebrews in the Holy Land, it was not that he did not love freedom; it was only that Something inside of him was compelling him to find God, and from what he knew at the time, the only place God was to be found was in Jerusalem. The strange thing is, of course, that it was true, only he went to the wrong part of Jerusalem at first, because he did not know of the other. So he went to the temple and learned the letter of truth, which "killeth."

But operating in his consciousness all the time that he was working and studying in the temple was this drive for truth, and even though he could not recognize it in the Master or in the Master's teachings, nevertheless, the drive for truth was there, and eventually he found it. He was led out of that temple; he was led out of the letter of truth into the experience.

But let us never forget that all those years of his freedom and the years of his life in Jerusalem, there was an activity going on in his consciousness driving him to truth, even to the extent of being willing to give up his freedom. There was something driving him on, and once that drive is there, it does not come by virtue of man: it comes by virtue of God. It will not lead us in a wrong direction. It is we who in our ignorance permit ourselves to go in a wrong direction; but ultimately It leads us to that which inwardly we are seeking, and that is God-realization. To each one of us, regardless of what path we are following on earth, the goal is God-realization.

The Freedom of the Infinite Way

No one who reads this *Letter* will ever rest until the goal is achieved, and that goal is God-realization. It is for this reason that in the message of the Infinite Way each one is not only free when he comes to it, he is just as free when and if he goes. No one is ever bound to this message by membership, obligation, duty, or for any other reason, because this message recognizes above all that no person is seeking this message: he is seeking God-realization, and if this message can be a help to him on the way, he is welcome to it. It was the way in which I came: and it is set forth as a help for all those who may be led to it, but for no other reason. It is not to bind anyone ever in a membership, a duty, or an obligation.

When the day comes when I am not visibly present, do not let anyone make you believe in the virtues of organizing this teaching, having memberships, and uniting to get greater benefits from it, because there are no benefits to be had from uniting or from memberships. The only uniting that gives any benefit to anyone is uniting with God. Your conscious oneness with God is your salvation. This message is intended to help those who are receptive and responsive to it, but to help them, not by taking them out of freedom, but by leaving them in their free-dom. Always remember this—and those of you who are very young, please remember it in the generations to come—when somebody tries to sell you on the idea of how wonderful it would be to unite to build a monument to the teacher, or to get a greater blessing from God for yourself.

There will be many good reasons offered why this should be done, but you have been taught in this message that the secret of life is consciousness, your individual consciousness. Your consciousness, in its oneness with God, is infinite and supreme—not your consciousness in union with other men and women: your consciousness in its oneness with God. We can unite in meditation and find a greater strength, but that uniting in meditation has no human obligation with it, none whatsoever.

Let this work forever result in your freedom and in the freedom of those who come to it, so that wherever there is a meditation oasis, be sure that everyone who comes to meditate in it is free to meditate in accordance with his spiritual leading. If he would like to sit in a chair, make him welcome; if he prefers a pillow on the floor, let him have that.

Sowing to the Spirit Leads to Ascension

All right, then, Easter is to be an experience, an experience of resurrection. It is an experience of complete freedom from every human limitation. We prepare for that experience every moment of our life. Just as in planting fruit trees, the goal is to have fruit, so the preparation for the ultimate experience of fruitage is the planting of the seed, the rain, the sunshine, the fertilizer.

So with us. Abiding in the word of scripture, letting the word abide in us, consciously renewing our understanding moment by moment, and abiding consciously in truth, we bring forth spiritual fruitage. Letting ourselves be mentally unconscious, we take in the seeds of the carnal mind, and the fruit that we bring forth is carnal. "For he that soweth to his flesh shall of the flesh reap corruption; but he that soweth to the Spirit shall of the Spirit reap life everlasting."[13]

Sowing is an activity of consciousness. We cannot sow without abiding in truth; we cannot sow without an activity of consciousness going on. Therefore, let us be careful that we are not letting the mind be idle, so that it takes in every seed that is blowing around in the air, but let us keep the mind active, abiding in the truth, so that we are sowing to the Spirit; and then on Easter, that is, at a particular day or moment, an experience of resurrection takes place.

It may not be on the day called Easter Day. Each one of us has his own Easter Day; each one of us has an actual moment of experience in which he is resurrected, in which the "old man" of us is dead, and there is a three-day period after which *I* raise up this temple again. And then there is the longer period of preparation for the final experience of ascension above mortality, ascension into Christhood, even while here on earth.

Let us always remember that since Jesus attained Christhood, he was imparting to us the truth that Christhood is the measure of our experience, our goal, our attainment. Once we have been touched, we never again can rest until we have attained it. True, for a long, long time, we are all going to say, "I do not claim to have fully attained, but I am going to repeat, day after day, that that attainment is my goal, and that I do know that I will attain it only by an activity of truth in my consciousness.

Across the Desk

Be a witness this Easter season to God's glory. Open your consciousness to that *I* within you which has been knocking, begging, and pleading for admittance that you may show forth

Its grace and the beginningless and endless nature of life: the life eternal, the life more abundant, more glorious, more joyous. That is our reason for being.

Joy to you this Easter and always.

Tape Recorded Excerpts
Prepared by the Editor

In London, during a class on the Resurrection, Joel said that his consciousness soared to such heights that he had no consciousness whatsoever of body. Following is an excerpt from that tape which emphasizes the role of body in our experience and gives new meaning to Easter:

Dominion over the Body

"You are not in your body. That may not seem at this moment to be of much importance, but sooner or later you will find that it is the ultimate secret of life . . . and the one that produces the greatest demonstration of spiritual living.

"We do not live in our bodies. You cannot find any of us from head to toe. We are not there, nor are we body. Therefore it is always wrong when feeling ill to say, 'I am ill,' for I am never ill. That body may be, but not I, not I for I am not in that body to be ill. I am nowhere around where the pain or discord is. I do not inhabit the body . . . I never was there. I live and move and have my being in God—not in a material concept, not in a tomb. I live and move and have my being in God, in Spirit, I dwell in the secret place of the most High. I abide in the word of God and the word of God abides in me—not in the body.

"There is no place in the body where you could hide the word of God. But the word of God does abide in you, and you abide in the word of God. When you begin to perceive that spiritually, you will be able to look at this body and say, "Now I perceive that I . . . was given dominion over this body. I was given dominion over everything on earth, beneath the earth, and above the earth. I have dominion over this body. I govern it, I feed it, I care for it. It is my possession. By realizing that, I take my body out of this world where it has been at the mercy of weather, climate, food and calendars that testify to the passing of time. I take my body out of the carnal mind by realizing that I was given charge of it—not to turn it over to calendars, to the control of winds and weather. No, I was given it to care for.

"*I,* the very Spirit of the Lord God, is the principle and the law unto my body. As long as I know that I am not in the body, but govern it, I have given my body to my divine Self for Its government. *I* does not have to control the body by conscious thinking or by psychological beliefs. *I* left to Itself governs the body. *I* knew enough to form this body; therefore *I* knows enough to govern this body and maintain and sustain it."

Joel S. Goldsmith. "The Secret of the Resurrection,"
The 1958 London Open Class. Reel 4, Side 1.

Chapter Five

Transforming the Unillumined Human Mind

We are born into a state of spiritual ignorance, and in that state we do not have the benefit of truth operating for us. It is for this reason that some of us come into the world physically or mentally handicapped, and it is possible for anything to happen to us of either a good or an evil nature.

Because personal experience is the result of what is taken into the mind, as long as our mind is the human mind with its good and evil, we will live the experience of the human mind, which is a false sense of mind, both good and evil. The mind, however, in and of itself, is neither good nor evil: it is merely an instrument of awareness.

A mind imbued with truth will bring forth harmony of mind, body, business, home, or family, but only in proportion to the degree in which that mind is stayed on truth. A mind imbued with ignorance, that is, one that accepts a materialistic view of life, must bring forth a life after its own image and likeness, which is also material, and therefore, both good and evil. Until we are led to some truth-teaching, however, we do not have the capacity to choose whether our mind is to be imbued with truth or whether it will remain under the domination of world beliefs. Up to that time we are in ignorance of the truth that our mind, when it is imbued with truth, will bring forth harmony, but when it is ignorant of truth and accepting the world's materialistic beliefs, it brings forth discord and inharmony.

Abiding in Truth Leads to the Illumined Consciousness

As we come to a truth-teaching, we learn that there is a truth which is contrary to human belief and also contrary to some orthodox religious teachings. First of all, we discover that there is no God sitting around in heaven worrying about whether we have an accident, become enmeshed in sin, or succumb to a disease. Our prayers to this unknown God are of no avail. Truth-teachings reveal that the reason these prayers have not been effective is because an individual does not know how to take dominion over his own life, does not know spiritual truth, and therefore has a life made up of some of the good beliefs of the world and some of the evil beliefs of the world.

Our first lessons in a truth-teaching should be for the purpose of keeping our mind filled with truth and, through knowing the Bible, keeping ourselves consciously aware of the revealed truths of spiritual teachings. Through this practice, it seems that we are changing the outward aspects of our life. Actually, we are not doing that at all. What we are doing is changing our state of consciousness, and it is this changed state of consciousness that produces harmony in our outer experience.

If our human consciousness were to remain at its present state of unawareness, because we have only dabbled in truth-teachings instead of making them an integral part of our consciousness, the only thing that would happen is that we would have a few more experiences of harmony rather than discord. What actually happens, however, when we abide in truth, when we live, move, and have our being in spiritual awareness, is that the human mind begins to lose its spiritual ignorance and darkness and begins to become illumined. In proportion as consciousness is illumined, the outer experience of life becomes spiritually harmonious.

This is especially true when we come to the message of the Infinite Way in which we are not so concerned with changing the immediate outward picture as we are with a transformation of consciousness. Of course healing of physical, mental, moral, or financial discords does take place because this is part of the signs following. But our major concern is in changing this state of unillumined consciousness to one of illumination, changing a darkened consciousness to one of light.

Where there is light, there is no darkness. Light and darkness cannot occupy the same space at the same time. Therefore, if we have an illumined consciousness, there is no darkness, and that means no sin, no disease, no death, no poverty.

Our responsibility on this path is to surrender our spiritual darkness to admit spiritual light and truth into consciousness until our consciousness is so illumined that the dark places of human experience evaporate, not only for us, but for those who touch our consciousness, because once light comes into our consciousness, we become the light of our world. We begin to see harmony taking place in our home, among our friends, in our community, and ultimately out in the world.

Then come the questions: How do I attain this light? How do I attain illumination? How do I make the transition from having a human mind to having that mind which was also in Christ Jesus? How do I have that mind which was in Buddha, Lao-tze, Moses, Elijah, Isaiah, John, or Paul? How do I attain that mind? The answer is found through a study of scripture. The scriptures of all the world reveal how that light is attained. First, however, we must discover what the light is and then set about learning how it is attained. In the Infinite Way, there are specific ways of bring this light to our consciousness.

No Mumbo Jumbo Affirmations

From the beginning of the introduction of truth-teachings into the world, a use has been made of affirmations, and often such affirmations are statements from scripture. This is, indeed, a good beginning. We must be careful, however, about the use of affirmations. If we take an affirmation, a statement of truth, or a Bible passage and repeat it over and over and over again, we are very apt to hypnotize ourselves and approach truth with blinders on, so that we are merely repeating an affirmation or a statement, and not really catching its meaning, believing that the repetition of those words is going to have some magical effect in our lives. Sometimes it does, but more often than not it proves to be only of temporary benefit because we have not caught the idea behind that statement. It is not the statement that has power: it is catching the idea that is embodied in the statement that is power.

To illustrate this, let me point out that in the Infinite Way writings very rarely is there just one Bible passage found at a time. Usually if I say, "For he performeth the thing that is appointed for me,"[1] very quickly thereafter I will say, "The Lord will perfect that which concerneth me,"[2] and then within a minute or two, "Greater is he that is in you, than he that is in the world."[3] I have not given just one particular statement to repeat and repeat and repeat until a person is hypnotized with it, but I have conveyed an idea to him. That idea is that there is a *He*. There is a *He* that performs that which is given him to do; there is a *He* that perfects that which concerns him: there is a *He* within him that is greater than he that is in the world.

Through this, all of a sudden the idea comes, "I am not alone: There is a *He*, and the *He* is within me, and that *He* is power." With that, the student has caught the entire idea of the passage, and now he is not depending on a mumbo jumbo affirmation to go out and do a miracle for him, nor is he dependent on some statement that he does not even understand.

The Inner and the Outer Self

Another passage of scripture that I use very often is "I and my Father are one."[4] Now, if we stop to analyze that statement, it is a foolish one. From every human standpoint, there is no sense to the statement that "I and my Father are one." If we think of our own fathers, we will know that I and my father are not one: there is my father and there is I. The mere fact that in this statement, we use the word "are," a plural verb, makes the whole thing unrealistic. We are saying that one is two or more. Therefore, if we were just to abide in the statement, "I and my Father are one," we would soon begin to question our own wisdom in believing that two can be one.

But let us take that now: "I and my Father are one." Yes, but the Master says, "My Father is greater than I."[5] That changes it a little bit, and so we have: "I and my Father are one," but "my Father is greater than I." Then he says, "The Father that dwelleth in me, he doeth the works"[6]; so it is not really one: it is two. There is the Father within me, and there is a "me." There is the "me" that is not doing the works, and there is the Father within me that is doing the works, and yet I have to see that "I and my Father are one." Now we really have something to think about, not just repeat statements, not vain repetitions, not just quote somebody else's words. We have something to ponder, something to take into our meditation.

When we take these statements into meditation—"I and my Father are one . . . . My Father is greater than I . . . . The Father that dwelleth in me, he doeth the works"—eventually it dawns in our consciousness that the real meaning is that there is an inner Being and an outer being; there is an inner Self and an outer self; and while these are one, just as the inside of the body and the outside of the body are one body, nevertheless, there are two different functions.

So we see that there is an inner Self to us, an inner Being which is God, and then there is this outer self which is the individual expression of God, or the son of God, and yet inseparable and indivisible. If we grasp that idea of oneness, we will be eternally free of this sense of duality, and we will be free of the egotism that believes that man is God, or that says, "I am God." We will be free of the false sense that we are out in this world alone, responsible for our own welfare, and we will catch an idea which will be embodied within us, and forever and forever it will be ours. It is not like an affirmation that we can forget, nor like an affirmation that we may not thoroughly understand. But by taking two, three, or four passages of scripture and putting them together, eventually an idea evolves, and once we have it, it is ours. We never again will be in ignorance on that particular subject.

With three or four months of this kind of work, students will know how to combine two, three, or four Bible passages on a particular subject and contemplate them until their real meaning is revealed and a measure of enlightenment attained.

How Scripture Is Used in
Developing an Idea in Consciousness

All the writings of the Infinite Way are based on scripture, and I would like to have it understood how these chapters based on Scripture are formed, how through this we obtain whatever measure of light there is to be obtained through these writings, and thereby go from the state of ignorance to the state of illumination.

In order to show how a chapter in one of the Infinite Way books is developed, which is much the same thing as forming an idea in consciousness, I quote from the first chapter of *Living the Infinite Way:*

There was a time when man was pure, spiritual being, when he lived entirely from within himself, when his thoughts always remained at the center of his being, and life flowed out from within— ideas came from within, means of action came from within, and whenever there was an apparent need, all that he had to do was to close his eyes,go within, and let it come forth into expression.

We have no actual knowledge of this period or of its ending, but we do know that the Bible symbolically relates the story of Adam and Eve who lived a divinely spiritual life without a problem, but who were compelled to leave the Garden of Eden and thereafter experienced all the troubles of human living—materialistic living. We are told that the reason for this fall from Grace was the acceptance of the belief in two powers—good and evil. It was an act of consciousness and, despite the commonly accepted theological interpretation, was not in any way related to sex.

The Garden of Eden episode contains a lesson in living for all of us. How often we feel that our lives are made or marred by some external act, but this is never true because it is always something that takes place within our consciousness that brings about the change for good or evil, and in the allegory of Adam and Eve, the downfall of man is explained as the acceptance of the belief in good and evil. [7]

In this chapter so far, I have tried to show that the discords of existence take place because of an act of consciousness, and in this case, it was the act of accepting the belief in two powers, the power of good and of evil. If we were to stop there, however, we might not clearly discern the nature of this lesson of Adam and Eve. It may not be entirely clear how Adam and Eve brought all of this trouble upon themselves and upon us by the acceptance of the belief of good and evil, so now we go on from there.

> Another symbolic story in scripture is that of the Prodigal Son. Here, the son of the king, who in and of himself was nothing, but who as the heir of the king was not only regal but wealthy, decided to cut himself off from the source of his good, that is, from his Father's house, his Father-consciousness. Taking the substance which he felt was his due, he began to live on that finite and limited amount that he had received. Living thus finitely, he cut himself off from his source. Whatever money he spent left him with that much less; every day of life he lived found him with a day less to live; every bit of strength or substance that he used found him with that much less, because he was using the substance that he had without being able to replenish it from the source from which he had cut himself off by his own act. [8]

Now we have two stories: one, Adam and Eve who cut themselves off from their source, from Eden, and the Prodigal Son who cut himself off from his source, the Father-consciousness. They did it by an act of their own consciousness. Ah, but we may not yet be convinced. Let us assume that we are a little hard or dull of perception, and we cannot quite see how Adam and Eve apply to us, or how the Prodigal Son applies to us, and so we go into a third biblical passage.

> That same principle is brought out in the lesson of the vine and the branches which the Master gave to his

disciples in the fifteenth chapter of John:

"I am the vine, ye are the branches: He that abideth in
me, and I in him, the same bringeth forth much fruit:
for without me ye can do nothing.
If a man abide not in me, he is cast forth as a branch,
and is withered; and men gather them, and cast them
into the fire, and they are burned."

Herein lies the essence of biblical wisdom: Cut off
from the vine, the branch withers, no longer having
access to the Source; cut off from the Father's house, or
Consciousness, the Prodigal consorts with the swine;
cut off from their source and expelled from the Garden
of Eden, Adam and Eve are compelled to live on their
own substance.[9]

With these three illustrations, is it not clear that if we were
to read these passages over two, three or four times, and then if
we were to sit in silence and in quiet for a little while and ponder them, eventually we would understand the essence which is
that if I am using up my substance, if I do not have the health
of God, the infinite supply of God, in some way, by an act of
consciousness, I have cut myself off from my source, the spiritual storehouse. Like the Prodigal Son, I must pick myself up
and go back to the Father's house; or if I am the branch of a tree
that has cut itself off from the vine, I must now, by an act of
consciousness, return to the Father's house, or reunite myself
with God.

Since this is an act of consciousness, I do not have to go out
and run off to India or Tibet; I do not have to look for holy
mountains; I do not have to look for holy synagogues or temples or teachers: I have to sit in quietness and by an act of con-

sciousness reunite myself by acknowledging; "I and my Father are one." I have to remember consciously, "Son, thou art ever with me, and all that I have is thine."[10]

Being Renewed by the Word

We do not use affirmations, but we take passages of Scripture and abide in them, and let them abide in us until the light of understanding dawns. Then we are no longer cut off; we are no longer separate or apart from our source; and from that time on, instead of using up so much life every day and running out of it by the time we have reached threescore years and ten, we are being renewed day by day. It makes no difference how much we use up in this hour. In a few minutes, it will be restored. It makes no difference how much we use up in a day, a night, or a year: it will always be restored because we are not cut off from our Father's house: we are consciously one. This oneness, however, is established only by an act of our consciousness. It is we who must consciously remember these passages of scripture and then realize that "I and my Father are one."

As we leave our homes in the morning, we do not go out as individuals separate and apart from God, but "I and my Father" go out together, because the Father is within us; the Father is closer to us than anything in this world.

After we have learned these Bible passages, when we recite one of them to ourselves, we do not repeat it over and over and over again mechanically. We try immediately to recall a second one and a third one that has somewhat the same meaning. This sequence of passages that will come to us shows that we have caught the idea, that we really understand what scripture is trying to reveal.

When we read the Bible with spiritual vision, we will see that the whole of it, from Genesis to Revelation, is trying to show us that the human race is cut off from God, and that our ultimate salvation is bound up in our return to the Father's house. But this return to the Father's house is not accomplished by the ceremonies, rituals, rites or holy days of an external religion. This return to the Father's house is attained only by an internal religion, a relationship between "I and my Father" that is established consciously within us.

It is reported that Dr. Jung, the noted psychiatrist, said that he had never had a patient over thirty-five years of age who was healed except through a return to religion—not the religion of orthodoxy, but one of the ancient, original religions. It was not a matter of going through the forms and ceremonies and rites of an external worship, but a return in consciousness to the original source.

Once we are adults and are living a life separate and apart from God, there is very little possibility of renewing our lives humanly. At thirty-five or forty, the harm to our life is already done, and there is very little chance of overcoming that harm unless it is through making that return journey, a conscious at-one-ment or oneness with the source. Then, it would make no difference if we were threescore years and ten, twenty, or thirty. If we actually made that contact with our source, "the years that the locust hath eaten"[11] would be restored to us. The lost years of sin, disease, and lack would all disappear from our experience, and we would have the opportunity of being reborn.

We must "die daily"[12] to that old man; we must be reborn; but that "dying" is an act that takes place in consciousness. Our consciousness is the point of contact between ourselves and our source. We take a book of spiritual wisdom, as we did with that chapter in *Living the Infinite Way,* and are very careful that we never believe that it is holy; but we take these passages as they are given in this chapter on "The Mystery of the Invisible" and read them over and over, until they are really part of us. Then ponder, meditate, cogitate until a light breaks within, and we say, "Oh, 'whereas I was blind, now I see.'[13] Now I understand the meaning of that passage; now it lives for me."

The Bread of the Word

A passage of truth, which is really understood, is bread, meat, wine, and water. It is your spiritual good, your spiritual medicine; it is your spiritual rejuvenation, your spiritual rebirthing. Every passage of Scripture that lives for you to the extent that you can say, "I catch it! I understand it; I grasp it," is a renewed life.

The Master said, "Man shall not live by bread alone, but by every word that proceedeth out of the mouth of God."[14] How many times is that passage used in our writings! How little of its real meaning we have grasped! If we could really catch what the Master is saying, our whole outlook on life would change. The Master does not say not to eat food; he does not tell us not to eat. That is part of our life; but he is revealing that man cannot live by bread alone, by food alone. There must be this transcendental Something, this oneness with God, this bread of life, this staff of life. That is why the Master prayed, "Give us this day our daily bread."[15]

Here again we have two passages to contemplate and ponder until we understand that Jesus meant that man shall not live by material food alone, but that God will "give us this day our daily bread"—the word of God. Man shall live "by every word that proceedeth out of the mouth of God." Every spiritual word is bread. When we begin to perceive that the spiritual word is bread, we will want as much of the spiritual word as we can possibly digest and assimilate.

Memorizing and Using Bible Passages

Students should work with Bible passages and, if they do not already know them, memorize them, utilize them, and above all, be sure that they do not use these passages merely as affirmations, declaring one statement over and over again in a hypnotic way. What students should do is to take a passage, then bring to conscious remembrance another similar passage, and if possible, a third one and a fourth one until the idea becomes clear. They will find that after that they are free on that particular subject. They can go on then to another group of biblical quotations presenting another principle, until it is completely clear that scripture really is the bread of life. We can live by scripture when it is known, when it is understood, and when it is embodied in our consciousness.

In all three illustrations given above, there is one spiritual lesson. When we are cut off from the source of our being, we are using up our own life, our own mind, strength, health, wisdom, guidance, and direction, and eventually we come to that period when we are withered. On the other hand, by maintaining our contact with the Vine, by maintaining our relationship as son or heir with the Father, or by remaining in Eden, in the kingdom of God, we draw on the infinite storehouse. This way leads to eternality, immortality, infinity, harmony, completeness, and perfection.

The Value of Living with Scripture

In studying the chapter in *Living the Infinite Way,* the student might think that I arranged the chapter that way, that there was some kind of a plan drawn, and that it was then written. Not so at all! That chapter is actually one of our class lessons, and it came out as spontaneously as this is coming out. Why? Because all the years of living with these passages of scripture, all these years of applying them makes it possible that at any given moment I can sit down and give a lesson like the one in that chapter, but only because after years and years of working with these passages they have become embodied in my consciousness, and that is what I am living on. That is what the Infinite Way is—nothing more nor less than scripture, but embodied and understood at least in a tiny measure.

Therefore, with these scriptural passages, whether a person has to give a lecture, a class, or write a book, it is very simple; but it is just as simple to handle family problems, business problems or legal problems by using them. In the Infinite Way we are working with business people on their problems; we are working with families on their marital problems. We are working with every kind of human problem and doing it with these passages of scripture forming the consciousness that produces the harmony.

Through Scripture the Mind Is Imbued with Truth

The human mind, when it is ignorant of all this scriptural truth, is the unillumined human mind that is made up of good and evil; but the same individual, embodying these spiritual truths, living with them, working with them, and applying them is no longer that unillumined human mind. That human mind is then imbued with spiritual truth and spiritual power.

The New English Bible[16] is a translation of the Bible into common English. It has been taken out of its old form, and all of these truths have been put into the language that we use in our everyday living just as I have used them in Infinite Way writings from the beginning. One of these passages, which I am sure was never clear before, all of a sudden comes to life. It says in plain English: "Stay here in this city until you are armed with power from above."[17] The Master was talking to his disciples and telling them not to be in a hurry to go out and preach this gospel, but to stay right there in their city and wait until the Spirit revealed Itself to them.

We can take that passage and interpret it in this way. Let me live my daily life just the way I am living it now; let me not plan or contemplate any changes, just stay where I am, doing what I am doing until I am imbued with spiritual power from on High. But while I am waiting, let me help this waiting period along a bit with my study, my meditations, my pondering of scripture, my praying daily for this spiritual bread.

We shall find, then, that what happens is that this gross mind with which we were born, this materialistic sense, which says that we live by money, by investments, by bread alone, by food or climate, less and less dominates our experience as it becomes more and more true that we live by these spiritual unfoldments. These comprise the vast majority of our experience, and the human modes and means of protection and security are lessened.

Our mind will become illumined, enlightened, and instructed in proportion as we grasp and discern the meaning of inspirational Bible passages, learn to live with them, practice and apply them in our daily experience. Let us take these next few months for the study and learning of these passages of scripture and this mode and means of application, and watch what it does to our experience and what it does to our own inner freedom. It is amazing how sometimes the grasping of a scriptural passage can remove a whole weight of fear from us.

Receiving the Bread from Heaven Through Listening

As we meditate, let us not be thinking but listening. We listen because we want to receive "the bread which cometh down from heaven."[18] That is the bread which unfolds to us from within our own being.

If we were to take that literally, we would be expecting bread to drop down from the skies. If we were just to repeat that thoughtlessly, we would, in some way or other, be wondering about this bread that is going to fall down out of the clouds. However, we are not going to stop with the statement, "the bread that cometh down from heaven." We are going to search for another statement that will clarify it: "The kingdom of God is within you."[19] Ah, then the kingdom of heaven is within us. The bread that we are waiting for is the bread that is to unfold from within us. In the very minute we stopped at that first passage, which indicated a heaven upstairs and a bread that is going to come down from there, instead of accepting it literally and repeating it, by letting thought go one step further, it comes to us, "The kingdom of God is within you." Therefore, the bread that is to come to us from heaven is the bread that is to come from the kingdom of God that is within us.

How that makes us jump forward! Does it not immediately bring to thought, "And we must open out a way for the imprisoned splendor to escape"[20]? What a difference there is in that first passage, "the bread that cometh down from heaven," and what it means to us now after two additional passages have come to us!

Immediately follows the passage, "I have meat to eat that ye know not of."[21] So we are waiting for the bread or meat that comes down from heaven, but the kingdom of God is within us. Therefore, we are waiting for the bread and the meat to come forth from within us, and that leads naturally right up to the truth that should any temptation present itself to us that we need anything—an idea, a dollar, a home, a job—we are going to answer it with "I have meat; I have bread; I have wine, I have inspiration; I have meat the world knows not of. I have a source of inspiration. I have my oneness with God. I have my supply within me. I have a supply within me that the world knows not of. Already the kingdom of God is established within me, the wholeness of God, the allness of God."

Then relax in that, and watch what happens in the outer experience.

Across the Desk

There are few Infinite Way students whose associates are only Infinite Way students. Most of us live and work with those who know nothing about spiritual truth and are not even interested in it. Although we may deplore this, actually this situation can be our opportunity. It is not an opportunity to tell them about truth, however, for we know that must observe secrecy about that. We must "be still and know."

And what is it we must know? We must know that God is the source of all life and that God is individual being, the *I* at the center of every individual. We recognize that *I* in everyone we meet. We know that "I and my Father are one," and in that oneness we are one with every individual with whom we come in contact. This recognition blesses those we meet and ensures a relationship of harmony.

Chapter Six

The Nonattachment of a Developed Spiritual Consciousness

The major function of the spirit of God, as it operates as individual spiritual consciousness, is to break the attachment of the human mind to form and effect. It acts as a law of nonattachment, so that the effect of the operation of the Spirit is that a person loses his fear of the destructive elements of human life and he also loses his love of those things that temporarily seem good, but which oftentimes may prove to be destructive. The activity of the Spirit destroys the love, hate, and fear of external appearances, external powers, and external laws, and a person who attains some measure of that Spirit finally is able to say to any problem, "Arise, take up thy bed,"[1] and thereby let go of the problem, realizing that there is no power in effect, no power in any external condition.

A person who has attained even a grain of spiritual consciousness can enjoy the things of this world but never be attached to them: never be willing to lie for them, steal, or cheat, but always able to enjoy them as they come into his experience normally and harmoniously, without loss or injury to another.

Sudden Illumination or Unfoldment

The question, then, is how to attain this consciousness. With all the reading and studying I have done and with the unfoldments and revelations that have been given me, I have found only one way, and that is a way that has been known and taught throughout all the ages. I am not now speaking of the experience which comes to certain individuals without their knowledge or without any apparent preparation by them on this plane for this experience but which comes as an act of divine Grace. Even those persons, however, were undoubtedly prepared in previous lives.

As you examine the life of some persons on this plane who have attained illumination, you may sometimes wonder why it is that one individual here or there, by some act of the grace of God, attained a spiritual consciousness that he has not deliberately and consciously tried to build. Such experiences and such individuals, however, are rare because usually spiritual consciousness is developed. The twelve disciples of the Master are examples of this truth. None of them received illumination wholly by a divine Grace as the Master did. Each one attained it through the instruction of the Master and evidently through obedience to the teachings that he gave them.

On the other hand, some few have had the experience of sudden illumination, some even in their childhood, and then those persons have gone out to become spiritual teachers and sometimes religious leaders. Their students, however, had to develop it, had to work with it, and it is because of their experience that we know there is only one way of developing spiritual consciousness. This one way has several different approaches, but fundamentally it is always the same way.

Establishing God As the Activity of Your Day

In the Old Testament, one of these approaches is given by the great prophet Isaiah, "Thou wilt keep him in perfect peace, whose mind is stayed on thee."[2] Keeping the mind stayed on God will eventually bring about a spiritualization of consciousness, but the measure of attainment of that consciousness is determined by the degree the mind is kept stayed on God. Another passage from Hebrew scripture is: "Trust in the Lord with all thine heart; and lean not unto thine own understanding. In all thy ways acknowledge him, and he shall direct thy paths."[3] Watch what would happen to you if you allowed yourself to lean not unto thine own understanding. You would relax and no longer struggle for understanding or attempt to use your own knowledge. Instead, you would acknowledge God in all your ways:

> I acknowledge that if it were not that the presence of God is making Itself felt, I would not wake up in the morning healthy, happy, and joyous.

> I acknowledge that this is the day the Lord has made, and this is the day that God governs. Therefore my activities throughout this day are under the government of God, under the jurisdiction of infinite Intelligence and divine Love. I cannot be capable of anything this day except that which is a showing forth of God's wisdom and God's love.

Can you imagine what would happen to you as you went through an entire day leaning not on your own understanding for whatever it is you are called upon to do, but remembering always that the presence of God in you is your wisdom, your intelligence, and your love; that the presence of God in you is your safety, your security, and your inner peace; that the presence of God within you is the cement of all your human relationships?

What is it that makes for harmony in human relationships? Is it not that spiritual bond that exists among all of us? There is only one thing that maintains real peace, only one thing that establishes a real relationship of love, only one thing that keeps a spirit of sharing as the motivating principle in your experiences with one another, and that is the presence of God.

If it were not for the presence of God, each one would be living his own life, responsible only to himself, not caring for anyone else and not sharing with anyone else, each one concerned only with getting, receiving, achieving. The presence of God in your midst changes that entire relationship of getting to one of sharing, one of communing, one of helping in whatever way the Spirit may direct. This spirit of love, harmony, peace, and prosperity can always be maintained by continuously recognizing the presence of God in the midst of you.

Keeping the Mind Stayed on God

Thou wilt keep him in perfect peace,
whose mind is stayed on thee.

Isaiah 26:3

Lean not unto thine own understanding. In all thy
ways acknowledge him, and he shall direct thy paths.

Proverbs 3:5,6

Man shall not live by bread alone, but by every word
that proceedeth out of the mouth of God.

Matthew 4:4

The use of those first two passages is a fulfillment of the third one. By living with the first two passages, you would demonstrate and prove that you are no longer living by means of your salary, by the food you eat, or the families you have, but now there is another factor that has entered your life, and that is a spiritual Grace which has come about because of your living with "every word that proceedeth out of the mouth of God." That word of God which you are entertaining in consciousness now becomes your substance and your staff of life on which you can lean.

Scripture fits into a pattern once you begin to understand that these passages from the Bible were given to you for the purpose of developing spiritual consciousness, testifying to what happens in the life of an individual when he has attained some measure of that spiritual light.

Repeating Words Can Be Hypnotic

There are several of the Hindu religious teachings which have a practice that they call *Ramnam*. The practice itself consists of a continuous repetition of the word God. Under that discipline, an individual, from waking in the morning until sleeping at night, repeats over and over and over, "God! God! God! God! God! God! God!" This becomes such a part of him that even when he is conducting his business, even when he is reading or studying, or regardless of what he may be doing physically or mentally, there is a little area of consciousness that is repeating over and over and over again, "God! God! God!" In other words, he is keeping alive in himself the conscious recognition of the presence of God.

There is, however, a danger in such a practice and that is that if one is not careful the repetition of the name can become hypnotic, and a person can really be led to believe that there is some power in the word God. I have seen too often that for some people who attempt this the whole of reality, the whole of the world, disappears and is replaced with a realm of fantasy because they become hypnotized through the repetition of a word.

There is a mystical Russian order that works from the same

premise only in a different form. They have a short prayer that is called "The Prayer of Jesus," which is a petitionary prayer, begging Jesus for mercy. They repeat this prayer over and over and over again, not only hundreds of times a day, but thousands of times. No matter what they are doing, there is an area in the mind in which this prayer of Jesus is being repeated, repeated, and repeated.

In spite of its good aspects, this, too, has the drawback of becoming hypnotic, hypnotizing a person to the extent that he is not thinking it any more. The purpose of it is good, just as the purpose of *Ramnam* is good, because the purpose is much the same as ours in the use of scriptural passages in the Infinite Way. With our use of scriptural passages, however, there is no possibility of any self-hypnosis or mesmeric sense taking place, because we do not fasten onto one particular word or passage and let it become hypnotic. We take the circumstance as it may arise in our day's experience and bring to conscious remembrance a passage that may apply to that particular situation. Then there is nothing hypnotic or mesmeric and none of the "vain repetitions"[4] the Master warned against.

Using Scriptural Passages in the Solution of Problems

If a particular problem presents itself to you that at the moment seems a little difficult, you can bring to conscious remembrance the words from the Psalmist that you know so well: "He performeth the thing that is appointed for me.[5] . . . The Lord will perfect that which concerneth me."[6] You can relax in the assurance that there is a "He" and that if you can be still, this He that is within you will supply you with the answer to this problem, or even do more than this, work it out for you.

At times you may be presented with problems that have to do with time and space, and immediately you know that you of your own self could never accomplish this within the time that is at hand or with the distance that is involved, and so you call to conscious remembrance the truth that there is a spiritual Presence that goes before you to make "the crooked places straight."[7] The spiritual Presence is not confined to time or space and can be instantaneously in any part of the globe at the same moment that you are thinking that this Presence goes before you to make straight the way.

Sometimes you may be involved in legal matters, and it is important to remember instantly that justice and truth are not qualities of man, but of God. To look to "man, whose breath is in his nostrils,"[8] for justice, for equity, for truth, or for love would be an error; it would be a sin. You have no right to expect truth from man, and you have no right to expect justice from man, for these are qualities and properties of God. Therefore, if you have to go into a court of law, go with the realization that God alone is the source of justice, God is the source of law, God is the means and mode and activity through which and as which truth and love appear. Then you will find that these qualities come through a judge, a jury, or witnesses, whereas left to "man, whose breath is in his nostrils," they could very well be withheld.

You can see that working this way is the very opposite of being hypnotized by a statement because in Infinite Way practice you are always alert for further truths or facets of truth that will apply to the situation with which you are faced.

Release from Fear, Hate, or Any Form of Attachment

The effect of bringing to conscious remembrance scriptural passages is to spiritualize the consciousness of the individual engaging in this activity. With this practice, the consciousness of an individual is transformed, so that ultimately he reaches that place where there is left in him no fear, no

hate, no love, and no attachment to the forms of life, but
there is now a breaking of all sense attachments. Do not misunderstand this. It does not mean that you lose your love for
your family or country or your sense of obligation to them. It
means that you are completely free of being unduly influenced by the emotions; you are free of the undue human
attachments that ultimately make a person become so hope-
lessly fearful, hateful, or loving that all reason is thrown aside,
and he becomes a victim of his own emotions, rather than
having dominion over everything that is on this earth, above
it, or beneath it.

Spiritual consciousness leads to the attainment of your
original God-given dominion. You were not meant to be a
victim of hate or fear; you were not meant to be a victim of
possessive love: you were meant to have dominion over these
things, so that you can handle each emotion and each situation as it arises, not with venom, not with partiality, but with
the justice that is not of man but of God.

The Master plainly indicated that he was not sent here to
be a judge over anybody. One of the effects of spiritual consciousness is to free you from sitting in judgment, and once
you have been released from sitting in judgment, you are able
to see the situation as it is, and deal with it intelligently.

The practice of bringing to conscious remembrance the
passage "The place whereon thou standest is holy ground"⁹ is
really enough to remove all fear, because no one can fear
when he is standing in the presence of God. That would be
an impossibility. You need no words: you need only the
assured feeling of the presence of God, and fear will depart,
even if you are in the lion's den, even if you are loose in a rub-
ber boat on the ocean, even if you are lost on the desert. If
you had the conscious presence of God, fear would depart.
No circumstance in life could frighten you if you were consciously aware of a spiritual Presence.

Spiritualized Consciousness Overcomes the World

You will notice how many passages of scripture are used in my writings and how they exemplify every one of the healing principles. So, too, you will see how they can be brought into use at each instant where some opposite thought or emotion might be, releasing and freeing you from what the Master called "this world."[10] He said, "I have overcome the world,"[11] and just as he overcame the world through his uplifted consciousness, so whatever measure of this world you overcome, you will overcome through your spiritualized consciousness, a consciousness that you can attain through the use and practice of scriptural passages. That is one way of developing spiritual consciousness.

Another way that is known today of releasing a person from attachment to this world and lifting consciousness is what in the Orient is called the *guru* system, that is, finding a teacher who has been released in some measure from attachment to this world and spending some time in the presence of his consciousness. That contact alone often brings release and brings Christ-realization to students. This system is practically unknown in the Occident, however, because there are very few teachers qualified to undertake this work. But there is a means of attaining this release through the use of scriptural passages, a method that is employed throughout the entire Infinite Way teaching.

As you read the Infinite Way writings or hear any of the tape recordings, you will note that the entire message evolves around scriptural passages. Each passage is elucidated in some way, so that the passage itself can bring a release or an awareness. When you repeat, "Thou couldest have no power at all against me, except it were given thee from above,"[12] do you not see that the only purpose there is in bringing that to conscious remembrance is that you may understand that whatever the particular Pilate is in your life—some disease, some sin, some false appetite, some person, some condition—you may instantly bring to remembrance, "Thou couldest have no power at all against me, except it were given thee from above."? In other words, only that which is ordained of God, only that which emanates from God, only a law that comes forth from God is power. If you can realize that, then when you are faced with material, mental, or legal laws, you can say to any of them, "'Thou couldest have no power at all against me, except it were given thee from above.' Unless you are ordained of God, you have no power. Only that which is of God is power."

You find that this practice will ultimately bring you a release from the fears and doubts and from the situations that loom as such big problems, and in the measure of your release you have overcome this world, or some facet or phase of this world.

When you study well the four Gospels, and note how the Master touched the leper, you have to ask yourself, "How dared he do this in the face of the belief in those days that this was the deadliest of diseases?" How dared he? Because he had overcome the fear that there is any external condition that could bring harm to his experience. He had overcome the fear that there was any power in anything external to himself.

The Invisible Power of Spiritual Consciousness

If you persist in fearing the things of this world or if you insist on unduly loving the things of this world, they are going to react upon you. The reaction will be an emanation of your own consciousness. Conversely, in the degree that you are not controlled by fear, by love, or by hate, but are controlled only by your realization of the presence of God, do you find, as Paul found, that "none of these things move me."[13]

You read in the papers and you hear on your radio or television the threats that are coming to the world from so many different directions, but the question is whether you as an individual are hearing them merely as a bit of recorded day-to-day history or whether you are permitting them to excite in you a fear. Are you listening to them and saying, "'None of these things move me.' I am merely seeing history instead of reading it a hundred years from now"?

A hundred years ago, people were going through experiences similar to those that we are having today. We read about their experiences with a measure of detachment and do not react as those who were going through them must have reacted at the time. If they could have gone through those experiences in the same way that we now read about them, as if they were just passing shadows in time and space, they would have found their freedom from them, as we can find our freedom from what we are going through today.

"None of these things move me." Why? There is a grace of God in operation. There is a grace of God, and this grace of God is molding every situation on earth today. We are evolving, and we have been evolving from prehistoric times to this present moment of civilization, where most of the responsible people on earth no longer want to resort to the use of force to settle arguments between nations or individuals, and even industry prefers to seek the settlement of industrial disputes at the bargaining table rather than to resort to court action.

Thus you find on every hand that there is an invisible force operating to free this world from its discords; but this invisible force is not something that operates of itself: this force operates by virtue of what is taking place in individual consciousness. There is nothing in time or space that is making associations with one another harmonious, loving, just, free—nothing! Whatever is operating is operating in your consciousness and mine.

Spiritual Consciousness Brings Freedom to the World

When Infinite Way students meet together, it is in a spirit of Grace, love, and cooperation; it is in a spirit of receiving the word of God from the consciousness of God. The function of the Infinite Way, however, is not merely to set up a group of people who prove that they can live together harmoniously on earth. Its function is to prove that the development of spiritual consciousness brings freedom to the entire world, and that by virtue of the degree of their attained consciousness they help to bring about nonattachment to the rest of this world.

Each student goes out into a home, into a business, or into a profession; but each one must carry with him the consciousness of the presence of God, this consciousness of one power, so that in whatever environment he may find himself, he is consciously realizing, "There is but one power functioning here, and it is the power of Spirit, the power of love—not the power of my human love for anybody. That is not great enough to remove a headache, but the power of the spirit of love which is of God, operating here in my consciousness, is a law of freedom unto individual consciousness." Wherever you go, you go with that recognition, thereby keeping your mind stayed on God, so that God may be the cement of the relationships wherever you are.

As you recall the consciousness of those great spiritual leaders who became imbued with the spirit of Truth and became a light to their world, remember that this is exactly the measure of the power of your consciousness in life. As long as you keep your mind stayed on God, as long as you acknowledge God in all your ways, you have within you the same Spirit, the same mind that was in Christ Jesus. Therefore, wherever you go, you are a benediction; you are a blessing to any individual, to any group, to any meeting—by the power of silence, not by the power of speech.

Let Truth Declare Itself in Demonstration

One of the saddest experiences that you will have in associating with those who have some metaphysical and spiritual background is to hear them mouth the great words of truth, the great passages of scripture. The longer the student has studied and the further advanced he may seem to be, the more irritating it is to hear him voicing these sacred passages of truth and of scripture, instead of holding them locked up tightly within himself until he is called upon to share them with someone who wants them, not voicing them for the purpose of showing how much he knows, not voicing them to those who cannot possibly have an interest in them or understand them, but voicing them only to those who can keep them locked up in the way the Master taught.

If you know any truth, keep it locked up within yourself; make it a secret sacred prayer, unless the opportunity comes when someone asks for spiritual wisdom. Then share what you have and be loving enough to share it simply, giving "milk"[14] to the babes and meat to those who seem to be sufficiently advanced for it.

You do not show forth the degree of your understanding by how much truth you voice, but by how much silence you can experience. It is only in silence that the works of the Spirit are accomplished. That is why a silent treatment is much more powerful than an oral treatment. An oral treatment is apt to hit up against the consciousness of an individual and bring about rebellion.

If you say to a person in pain, "Oh, disease has no power," you can almost feel him bristle as he replies, "No? I wish you were suffering this pain." So your statement has not only not blessed the person, but it has antagonized him and has been a barrier to his healing. If instead, you had simply said, "I will be glad to help you; I will pray"; and then, in your silence realized God alone as power, you would have aroused no mental reaction from your patient, and there might have been some measure of receptivity to it.

In healing work or in your associations in your office, school, or business you will find that if you never voice your spiritual convictions but keep them locked up and spiritually realize them silently, you will be a tremendous influence wherever you are. By voicing truth, you not only arouse antagonism, but you might even arouse some suspicions as to your sanity, and rightly so, because almost every spiritual truth seems like insanity to the human mind. Paul recognized that when he said, "The natural man receiveth not the things of the Spirit of God: for they are foolishness unto him."[15] Yet how many of our metaphysical and spiritual students go around mouthing spiritual truths to the human ear, to which they are foolishness and insanity.

In my mail one student wrote telling me how she had said to her doctor, "Oh, I know this disease is not real." A doctor is hardly the person to tell that to, because he is undoubtedly spending his entire life trying to prove the reality of disease and to heal it.

The Power of Silence

But think! Think what a power you could be if you could learn the value of silence, an outer silence, but not an inner one. Inwardly you would be knowing the truth; inwardly you would be keeping your mind stayed on God; inwardly you would be bringing to conscious remembrance all the tremendous passages given us by such great spiritual lights as Christ Jesus and some of the Hebrew masters. To abide with these great truths and let these be within you would be truly a thundering of the silence. The silence would thunder throughout human consciousness, and only that silence is power.

When words are spoken in teaching, the only reason they have power is because of the silence that went before and the silence in which they are received. This is especially true of an Infinite Way meeting. If students go to a meeting having had a period of meditation and inner silence, they go with power to give and to receive, but it is only because of that period of silence which is like a vacuum into which the spirit of God is invited to enter and the word of God to express itself. Only in quietness and in confidence is that peace found.

Only in quietness and in confidence does a treatment function. A treatment does not function through a mind that is in fear of the condition that is being treated or fears for the person who is being treated. A treatment can function only in silence, in stillness, in an inner peace, and that is why only those should be engaged in the work who have found some measure of inner stillness and inner peace. The words themselves are not power: it is the consciousness through which the words come that is the power, and that consciousness is a consciousness of stillness, of silence, of inner peace, and of an inner Grace.

Morning, noon, and night, carry with you this truth: *"I* am with you." As you walk or drive along the street, you may at first have the feeling of being there alone, and this puts all the responsibility on your shoulders, but as you consciously bring to remembrance, *"I* am with you," the shoulders drop back a little and a relaxing comes. *"I* am with you, walking along the street, driving in the car, up in the plane, or down in the submarine. Wherever you are, *I AM. I* am with you."

That *I AM* is God: infinite power, infinite supply, divine love; and just to know, *"I* am with you," is enough to ensure that every need will be fulfilled at every moment. That *I AM* that is with you is the spirit of the Lord, the consciousness of the presence of God.

Across the Desk

Truth is presented in many ways so that it may reach the understanding of those who are in different stages of consciousness. The Infinite Way is based upon certain principles which, understood and practiced, lead to an awareness of truth. This really is a working way, for we work with a specific principle until it seems to become part of us, and then go on to another one. This procedure gives us a solid foundation in truth.

However, we have all found that as we study, our consciousness seems to widen and our understanding of truth to deepen. We have probably all had the experience of going to a book we haven't studied for some time and reading a familiar sentence or paragraph with a sudden surprise, for we see a meaning in it far beyond the one we originally saw. For this reason it is illuminating to go back to books and tape recordings that we think are so familiar we could quote them word for word, because with the increased understanding that comes to us with our study we may find new facets revealed on some one principle.

Tape Recorded Excerpts
Prepared by the Editor

God As One

"For at least a year, remember that God is one. Then you can take a word like "power": God is one power. If God is one, is there a power to be feared? Is there a power in thought or thing to be feared if God is the only power? . . . That, you have to bring to your conscious realization every day for a long while until it is established in you that God is one. . . . If God is the creative principle of all that exists, is there another creator? No. Is there a dangerous creation or a destructive creation? No, all that you are called upon to do is to know that God is one. . . .

"If you study the correct letter of truth and come into the awareness that God is one, not One over something else, not One protecting something else, and not One doing something to something else but One, . . . that itself would be a treatment—just the realization that God is one.

"It may be that you are in too much pain to think those three words. If so, you can shorten them to two, and almost anyone, even in pain, ought to be able to stand still long enough to give a treatment of two words, and the two words are: God is. If God is, everything else 'ain't.' . . . One of these days, you are going to realize that if God is, you haven't another trouble in the world. Your only trouble is the moment you doubt that God is, that moment you feel that God is not, the moment that you doubt a God. With God, who has to fear anything? Who has to treat anything? Who has to pray about anything? It is God's function to know your need; it is God's function to fill your need.

"If you accept the fact that God alone is one, one power, and everything else that claims to be power is but a shadow, a belief, a nothingness, then you can stand in your oneness and look right out at any form or phase of what the world calls error and recognize it for what it is, nothingness."

Joel S. Goldsmith. "God is One: One Power, One Life, One, One, One," *The Second 1956 Steinway Hall Closed Class,* Reel 1, Side 1.

Chapter Seven

Except the Lord
Build the House

A real student of the Infinite Way feels that there is nothing more important in life than the development of spiritual consciousness, getting to know God and living the life of prayer, meditation, and communion with God. Such a student soon learns that there is rich fruitage as a result of living in this way. There is better health and more abundant supply; there is greater success in human activities; there are greater capacities revealed—mental, moral, and physical—in students who really work and live with this message.

Even though students realize that and see the outer fruitage, many of them are never satisfied until they have gone a long, long way on the spiritual path developing their own inner capacities. If a person feels that way, what is more natural than to want to share the message with a neighbor, a friend, or a relative? What is more natural than to help someone else find his spiritual source? What is more natural than to want to send one's children out into the world imbued with the spirit of God? There surely cannot be an adult student of the Infinite Way who does not feel that the greatest gift he could give his child would be a knowledge of God, an acquaintanceship with God, and an ability to commune with God.

The Fruitage of Conscious Union with God

When a man lives consciously one with his source, he bears rich fruitage in health, harmony, inner peace, joy, prosperity, and all kinds of human relationships, not by virtue of himself, but because the grace of God hangs rich fruitage on him in the form of supply, health, home, and happy relationships. He is merely the place through which God is expressing His infinite abundance of all things.

We have had years of witnessing what happens to those who live consciously one with God. Looking out at this human scene, we know that human beings living separate and apart from their conscious union with God are sick or well, have accidents or do not have them, are rich or poor, are happy or unhappy, successful or unsuccessful, and without much control over which it is going to be, because a human being has no control over outer circumstances. The only control or dominion there is, is by virtue of one's union with God, one's conscious oneness with God.

These things we have known, and the entire teaching of the Infinite Way reveals this, and then shows how a person may reestablish contact with his source. It is dedicated to revealing once again the principle of life, which is that conscious union with God brings forth rich fruitage, whereas the sense of separation from God results in sin, disease, false appetite, lack, limitation, disaster, and accident, and then, devotes itself from there on to showing how, through abiding in the word of God, we may become reestablished in God.

Reestablishing Oneness Through the Word

The way to oneness, to conscious union with God, is through the word of God. It is the word of God maintained in consciousness, lived with, dwelt upon, abided in that ultimately restores that conscious union. The consciousness of truth is the connecting link between man and God that makes them one. Without the word of God consciously maintained in consciousness, there is no contact with God, and man and God cease being one and become two. They are separated to such an extent that the Master says that man cut off from his source withers and dies.

We know now that only through the consciousness of truth are we reestablished as children of God. Paul said it this way: "For as many as are led by the spirit of God, they are the sons of God."[1] The spirit of God is the consciousness of God. If the consciousness of God dwells in us, then are we children of God, "and if children, then heirs; heirs of God, and joint-heirs with Christ."[2] If the consciousness of God does not dwell in us, we are like a branch that is cut off. Every word of God that is entertained in our consciousness is our connecting link with our Source and the means whereby we ultimately bear fruit richly.

All the scriptures of the world reveal this same principle. The Hebrew scripture, the Christian testament, the Hindu and the Buddhist teachings all emphasize this same truth: if we have the word of God abiding in us, we have spiritual riches, abundance, and freedom.

Letting God Build Our Day

In the Hebrew testament we read, "Except the Lord build the house, they labour in vain that build it."[3] How can we have any awareness of the Lord building a house for us except through our consciousness? And how can we have the Lord build a house for us if we are looking to our parents or our grandparents to build it? How can we bring any good into our experience through the Lord if we are looking to "man, whose breath is in his nostrils,"[4] or to "princes."[5] Therefore, if we are to benefit from the house that the Lord builds for us, is it not clear that we must be looking to the Lord? And what means have we of looking to the Lord except through an activity of our own consciousness?

Let us suppose that it is early in the morning, and I am now looking to the Lord to prosper my day, to make it happy, healthy, free of accidents, sin, and free of false appetites. What must I do? The first and more important thing is to realize:

> Except the Lord build this day, this day will
> not be spiritually fruitful. Except the Lord build this
> day, I will not be prospered, I will not be successful,
> I will not be governed by divine Intelligence.
> But if I look to the Lord to build this day,
> I will have the grace of God with me,
> the peace of God and the presence of God. I will
> have His wisdom, and since His wisdom is infinite,
> why should I look to my wisdom?

But if I do not begin my morning in that realization that His wisdom is infinite and is within me, that the kingdom of God is within me, and that His wisdom goes before me to make "the crooked places straight,"[6] how can I expect to find that guidance and direction with me during the day?

Suppose we were to leave home and forget to take our wallet with us. We would not then have carfare, lunch money, or any other money that we might need during the day. So, too, when we begin our day and leave God somewhere up in a heaven, we are going through the day without God and will come to bedtime frustrated, unsuccessful, unhappy, and not at peace. But when we begin our day with the realization that except the Lord build this day, we will be laboring in vain, we have laid the foundation for a fruitful day. Therefore, we begin our day in such a way that it is built on the rock of the word of God, consciously remembered.

Solving Problems with Scripture

Sometime or other in the day a problem arises, one that for a moment has us baffled or frustrated. But now we are living not by our own wisdom, and we bring to conscious remembrance some bit of spiritual wisdom, such as, not by might, nor by power, but by the spirit of God. So we relax because this problem is not solved by might or by power, but by resting in God. Now we are not living separate and apart from God-presence and God-power: we are living by every word that proceeds out of the mouth of God.

Every chapter of the Infinite Way books is built around Bible passages as was explained in the May *Letter*. In fact, I do not know of a single chapter in the writings that is not developed from one or more Bible passages. The principles set forth in these chapters came to me by revelation, and then I found that they were in scripture, but there they are veiled and hidden so that the mass of people of this world do not really know that the Bible is the book of life. True, it is called that, and everyone knows that it is the book of life, but it is not the book of life they live by. Why? Because it is hidden, it is veiled, and although we read, "Except the Lord build the house, they labour in vain that build it," we have not been told that that passage, taken into our consciousness and lived with, will actually build a house for us. It will set a table for us in the wilderness; it will turn our failure into success.

Individual Consciousness As the Temple of God

House, church, temple, synagogue—these are no longer words referring to material edifices. House, church, temple, synagogue now refer to our consciousness, individual consciousness. Our consciousness is the temple of God, and since we are consciousness, we are the temple of God. "Know ye not that ye are the temple of God, and that the Spirit of God dwelleth in you?[7]. . . Know ye not that your body is the temple of the Holy Ghost which is in you? . . . Therefore, glorify God in your body."[8]

> God is the spirit that animates my body.
> God breathes His life into me as my life,
> so that my very life is the temple of God.
> My soul is the temple of God; my being is the temple
> of God; and even my body is the temple of God.
> God, Spirit, animates my body.

> *I* the spirit of God in me, am the life; *I* am life
> eternal, *I* am the blood and the bones. *I*, the spirit of
> God, animate my being and body from head to foot.

> Because of my consciousness of my oneness
> with God, I am united to the entire source and
> creative being of life, God.

While it is true that we are one with the Father, that we are the temple of God, and even our body is the temple of God, this is of no value or benefit in our life, except through our conscious knowing it. Therefore, let us turn now from our ignorance of God, man, being, and body, and consciously know the truth.

> Here where I am, God is, for I am the temple of
> God. I am the church; I am the synagogue; I am the
> holy mountain, for the kingdom of God is within
> me. As the temple of God, God fills me:
> Soul, being, and body.

> I am now consciously uniting myself with God. I have
> been one with God since "before Abraham was," [9]

but it has been of no benefit to me until
this moment when I consciously open myself to the
inflow and the experience of God.

God has built me and all that has to do with me.
God has built even my body.
No human being knows how to build a body.
It is God that builds the temple of this body.

God has built my home. It is God's holy temple,
and because of omnipresence,
God fills my home,
every nook and cranny of it. Therefore, nothing can
enter my home that "defileth . . . or maketh a lie." [10]

God has made my marriage; therefore my marriage is
the temple of God, and that which
God has united, no man can break asunder.

God has built my business; therefore my business is
the temple of God. God is the bread, the meat, the
wine, and the water of my business which is erected
and dedicated to God: to good, to service,
to quality, to the benefit of mankind.

It makes no difference what our business is—grocery business, church business, or a plantation business. When its purpose is to serve mankind, it is the business of God, and God is
in that business. Nothing can enter that business that can defile
or make a lie. This is the truth about the steamship business;
this is the truth about the banking business; this is the truth
about all business that is erected and dedicated to the service
and the benefit of mankind, because in serving mankind we are
serving God.

Bringing God into Every Experience

What has happened to our governments, our churches, our homes, our marriages, our families, our business that they are in such chaos except that God has been left out? "Except the Lord build the house, they labour in vain that build it" has been forgotten, and now, in order that "the years that the locust hath eaten"[11] may be restored, in order that we may resurrect our body, our home, our marriage, our business, we must turn and live, because God has no pleasure in our failure. God has no pleasure in the failure of our business, our marriage, or our home, any more than God has any pleasure in the failure of our body to show forth the glory of God. Our body was meant to show forth God's glory.

> Why were we created? We were created in the image
> and likeness of God to show forth God's glory, God's
> bounty, God's grace, God's peace. God has given us
> His peace, but to enjoy it, we must know this.
>
> God has given me life. It is God's life I am living
> because God could only give me His life. God has
> given me His peace, so that I may have peace.
>
> God has built this temple of my body in which He
> may dwell, in which His life may dwell. Therefore,
> my body must be a fitting temple for the Holy
> Ghost, for the spirit of God. God has built this entire
> universe to show forth His glory.
> God has built business, industry, art, literature,
> religion that God's glory may be shown forth.

As long as we are relying on human relationships for our good, we are not permitting God to build our life in order that it may function harmoniously. Our real life is lived in the consciousness of God's presence. Our hope, faith, and dependence must not be upon one another, but upon the spirit of God that indwells us. We are created equal in the sight of God, regardless of race or religion, but we maintain that equality only by maintaining the consciousness of God's presence within. God has not removed Himself from us. Though we may have kept God separate and apart from our life, our body, our business, or our family, in the moment that we turn, as the Prodigal turned even in his deepest extremity, in the moment that we turn and recognize God within, that Spirit takes over.

> God built the temple of the being that I am: the
> temple of my body, my home, my family, my
> business, my marriage. I accept God as the very
> cement that holds together every department of the
> edifice of my life. I seek only to glorify God.
> I let God fill every crevice of this activity of my
> business, art, or profession to show forth
> God's glory and to bless mankind.

We must consciously bring God into every avenue of our experience so that we make of ourselves what we originally were, the temple of God. We must make of our household, our marriage, our family, and our business the temple of God.

In serving even "one of the least of these"[12] with beauty, service, art, wisdom, grace, we are serving God. Every beggar that comes to our door to be fed by us is our service to God. Every worthwhile product sent forth from our shop dedicated to the service of God is a blessing to man and is under God's grace.

Living with Scripture

No one out in the world has told us that when we read "not by might, nor by power, but by my spirit,"[13] we are being given a principle of life. The very moment we can relax in the realization, "Wait a minute! Wait a minute! This is not my might or my power; this has to be done through the spirit of God," we can watch our problems being met by It.

How frequently are these passages from scripture quoted in the Infinite Way writings: "Greater is he that is in you, than he that is in the world.[14] . . . He performeth the thing that is appointed for me.[15]. . . The Lord will perfect that which concerneth me."[16] That is because these biblical quotations are not just poetic statements of scripture; these are not just beautiful passages: these are actually the word of God, that by which man should be living, so that regardless of what problems a person faces, he can turn within and remember:

> "Greater is he that is in you,
> than he that is in the world. . . .
> The Lord will perfect that which concerneth me. . .
> not by might, nor by power, but by my spirit,"
> by His own Spirit.

> I am the branch on which He hangs the fruit.
> I do not have to go out and struggle for fruit.
> I have to be at peace within myself in the realization
> that God is hanging fruit on me: fruit of a physical,
> mental, moral, or financial nature. I am that place
> where God shines through. Just as "the heavens
> declare the glory of God; and the firmament
> sheweth his handywork,"[17] so am I that place through
> which God reveals Himself: His Grace,
> His bounty, and His wisdom.

Founded on the word of God by which we live, such meditations flow forth spontaneously. As we are fed by those words, we are given the spiritual strength to go out into this world and perform that which is given us to do or to be the instrument through which it is performed. Without these scriptural gems, we do not have the word of God. Merely reading them in a book does not do the work for us, nor does hearing them in a lecture or having them repeated to us in a class. We have to take them into our consciousness, live with them, apply them to the problems of the day, and be ready to receive whichever of these is necessary at a given moment. But how can we do this if we do not know them, if we have not learned them?

By the time we have twenty or thirty scriptural quotations established in our consciousness, we shall find that there will not be a problem of our own, of our neighbor, or of our friends for which we shall not instantly have the right word of God with which to help meet the problem.

Most students have had the experience at some time during our classes of having healings take place right in a meeting, having their lives changed, having whole new experiences come to them. What brought it about except the word of God in consciousness? Take the word of God out of the consciousness of the teacher and how would any meetings he conducts be any different from that of a vaudeville actor sitting in front of an audience? It is the word of God that has become established in the teacher's consciousness, with which he looks out at the students, through which he sees them, and which he applies to every problem that he is aware of among them. It is only the word of God that has been established in him that makes him any different from anybody else walking up and down the street, and it is the word of God established in us that will set us apart from other people.

The Permanence of Freedom and Equality Is Based on the Word

According to the Declaration of Independence, we are all born equal, but how unequal do we become as we grow older.

Nothing can ever establish equality for us externally. Not all the laws of equality that can be thought up and passed can make us equal. Nobody can give us equality. Laws might give us the privilege of voting, but through our own lethargy that privilege can be taken from us at any time. Furthermore, the privilege of voting is not always such a great privilege because the candidates for whom we have to vote are given us, and sometimes there is not much of a choice. Let us not think for a single moment that anyone can legislate equality, nor believe that anyone can legislate freedom. Freedom can be taken away very fast from those who do not understand the real nature of freedom and equality.

No one can take equality or freedom away from us, however, if we have the word of God abiding in us. If we have the spirit of God in us, nobody can take advantage of us, nor can anybody bind us. Nothing like that can happen. But we must have the spirit of God dwelling in us, the word of God abiding in us. This gives us equality and freedom.

If we turn back in history to the days of the Hebrews around the time of the Caesars, we can see how much better they were treated than the other slaves, the special privileges they were given that others were not given. There is only one reason for this: they lived with the word of God; scripture was their meat and drink, even if they did not understand it and even if their church, at times, was very wicked. The truth of scripture was ingrained in their consciousness; they bound it on their arm; they put it on the gateposts of their homes so that no matter where they looked they were looking at the word of God.

Even though a thousand may fall at our left and ten thousand at our right, it will not come near our dwelling place if we are dwelling in the word of God and if we are letting the word of God dwell in us. If we live this way and follow a program such as is set forth in this *Letter* for the next eight or twelve weeks, we can see the difference that it will make in our own experience: in our inner and our outer experience.

Attain the Consciousness of God's Presence Before Leaving for the Work of the Day

When Jesus was leaving his disciples after the crucifixion and just at the time of the ascension, he left a message to the effect that they should stay in the city until they were armed with power from above. He had told them to go out and preach the Gospel and heal the sick, but his last admonition was for them to stay in the city until they were armed with power from above. This is what I have been trying to say to our students for years: Do not leave your homes in the morning, even if you find you have to get up an hour earlier, until you have the feeling that you can leave with the power and the presence of God; until you feel, through your meditation, that you have the spirit of God dwelling in you, that you have the assurance from within, "Go ahead. My Presence goes before you. *I* go before you to make the way straight.

Then when students leave their homes, they can leave relaxed because they will understand why the Hebrew prophet said, "Be strong and courageous, be not afraid nor dismayed. . . . With him is an arm of flesh; but with us is the Lord our God to help us."[18] They will leave their homes with the feeling:

> I need not fear. Not all the weapons the
> world has amount to a hill of beans,
> for I am going forth empowered with the
> spirit of God; I am going in God's grace.
> I have been given an inner assurance
> that the Presence goes with me.

If we attain the consciousness of God's presence, our fears are over, our worries are over, our doubts are over. It does not mean that we will not have some problems to meet. Furthermore, should the day ever come when all our problems are met, others will be coming to us with their problems, and these problems will be just as serious and just as much of a challenge to us as our own, because by that time we will have learned that there is only one Self, and that as long as anyone else is suffering so, too, are we suffering. Therefore, we must help; we must be the light of the world; but we cannot be that of ourselves. It is not given to man to be the light of the world except by the grace of God.

Helping Children Establish Themselves in the Presence

Those who have children or grandchildren around them and who understand this principle will not let their children leave home in the morning until they have shared with them some simple quotation and given it to them to remember throughout the day, whether at play or at school.

Give a child only one biblical passage and remind him several times a day to use it, or ask him, "Have you used it? Do you remember it?" It is the parent's function to instill that spiritual wisdom gently, not by force, not by threats, and not by bribery, but by gentleness and love. Let the child forget it a hundred times—it makes no difference. Remind him the hundred first time. Eventually he will remember it, and he will remember a second one and a third one. It will not take a child many months before he will be reminding you of scriptural truths and passages; and then you will see what the power of a child is when he is imbued with spiritual truth.

Even if a Sunday School teacher could give your child a passage to memorize on Sunday, what happens on Monday, Tuesday, or Wednesday? Somebody has to show that child, even as you have to be shown as an adult, how to use, how to apply, and how to remember biblical passages, until these spiritual truths become flesh of your flesh, bone of your bone, and blood of your blood. They become so much a part of you that you can literally say, "I am not living any more by external means. It seems that the word of God in me is living my life."

Universality of the Truth of Scripture

As some of these passages become a part of your consciousness, you will begin to note how world scripture all fits into the same pattern. You will find passages in the Old Testament, and then you will find confirming passages in the New Testament, and if you should turn to any of the Oriental scriptures, you would find similar passages in them and you would say, "Oh, now I see that truth is one." For example, the Golden Rule, "Do unto others as you would have others do unto you," appears in scripture in manuscript form, 1500 B.C., 1000 B.C., 800 B.C., 700 B.C., 400 B.C. It appears in the scriptures of India, Egypt, China, and Africa. Every part of the world has that particular scripture.

So you will find, as you go along, that you will not have just one passage of scripture, but when you see "Except the Lord build the house" in the Hebrew scripture, you will turn to the New Testament and you will read, "I live; yet not I, but Christ liveth in me,"[19] or you will see "Greater is he that is in you, than he that is in the world"; or "He performeth the thing that is appointed for me."

You will not be limited to one quotation, which would become stale by using it as an affirmation, but every quotation will be alive because it will bring to conscious remembrance all the similar statements. Gradually you will find that you have spiritual food, spiritual drink, and spiritual wine, and all of that will be the word of God which you will be entertaining in your consciousness.

The Word As a Connecting Link

Remember that the word of truth in your consciousness is the connecting link between you and God. Leave the word of truth out of your consciousness, and you have no contact with God. You are living a human life that is lived on a merry-go-round; but the moment you begin to maintain truth in your consciousness, you are maintaining your contact with your spiritual Source, and then you are fed from within, prospered from within, instructed from within, and healed from within. Everything comes from within, but remember it does not come from within your flesh and blood: it comes from the word of truth within which you have established in your consciousness.

When you leave your home in the morning, even if you find that you are not fully established in the conviction that there is a Presence within you, get as close to that realization as you can and then leave home with the word of truth in your consciousness to do the rest. But use whatever opportunities you have during the day, either at mealtime or when you go to the rest room, to give up again your earthly struggles and human problems for at least long enough to go back into these scriptural passages for three, five, or ten minutes—whatever time you have available.

It will not take more than a couple of months to find what a change has taken place in your life, once this has become the fabric of your life. Also, you will see the change it makes in your home without ever uttering a word of truth, without ever having to voice truth to anybody who may not wish to hear it, but just by keeping it locked up within you. You do not have to let anyone know you are praying or knowing the truth. When you do this in secret, within yourself, it will be shouted from the housetops.

In the days to come, the teaching of spiritual wisdom will not mean being on a platform preaching. It will mean living the truth and showing forth by our lives its value, and then when anyone asks a question, being able to answer his question and teach him. In the same way, in the days to come there will be no practitioners as such, because anyone who abides with these words of truth long enough will be a healer, and he will do healing work for his own home and his neighborhood so that it will not be necessary for staffs of practitioners to be maintained. We hope to see this come into fruition and be established in the consciousness of the next generation through this scriptural work.

Peace, the Fruitage of Love

It is this next generation and the one after that that will carry the burden of establishing peace and prosperity on earth. Our world has become debt-ridden; every nation on the face of the globe is practically bankrupt. So we are handing down to the next generation the debts that we have created and the obligation to try to find a way to liquidate those debts. The debt is not only a debt of money. The nations of the world are leaving a heritage of dishonor: dishonored agreements among nations, dishonored obligations from one nation to another. The least we can do, therefore, is to try to hand down to this next generation some measure of a spiritual heritage with which to meet the problems that we have put on their shoulders because those problems are not going to be surmounted by human means.

Ever since World Wars I and II, I have said many, many times that neither the League of Nations, the United Nations, nor any other organization of people is going to establish peace on earth or fellowship. Those things cannot be legislated and neither can they be organized; they must come forth from man's consciousness of good; and if he has not a consciousness of good, it will not take place. The tendency is to look too much to organizations for freedom and for peace. It cannot come that way! That is not the way.

The way peace is to come is exactly in the same way as it is to come in your life individually or mine, or into our lives collectively: through love. Love is not an emotion; love is not a statement: love is an act, and the only way we love is by action. The only evidence there is that there is any love among us is through action. If we respect each other, if we help each other to the extent of our capacity, if we forgive each other our faults, we are loving. If we do not do these things, we are not. If we are upholding our community, if we are maintaining our Community Chest funds and other benevolences, we are loving our neighbor as ourselves; but if we think we are too spiritual to help them at their level of needing help, we are just voicing words, and we are not doing what needs to be done.

So it is that love is the only thing that is going to settle the problems of life. But how can love be instilled except through the word of God? People have tried to instill it in schools; they have tried to teach that a person should be honest by repeating the words, "Honesty is the best policy," but honesty is not learned that way. For centuries, efforts have been made to instill honesty and integrity through obedience to the Ten Commandments. Not much progress has been made.

Integrity, loyalty, fidelity, justice, and charity are instilled through the word of God. Nobody could live with these scriptural truths in consciousness and live in violation of them. It can be done, of course, as it is out in the world, when a person merely learns scripture as quotations to use in speeches or to use in a sermon on Sunday, while the congregation is dozing or looking around to see if everybody else has her new hat on.

The proper understanding of scripture, which comes when an individual takes it into his consciousness, lives with it, and applies it to daily living, transforms consciousness and makes it impossible for a person to live other than in harmony with the truths of scripture. In other words, we would soon find that we must either get rid of scripture or get rid of the negative type of living in which we may have heretofore indulged. Both cannot exist together. There is no room for hypocrisy among those who take scripture as a way of life, who apply these inspirational passages in their daily living, not for the purpose of taking advantage of anyone, but merely to be a light unto the world, showing forth God's grace.

As you bring some passage of scripture to mind, pause for a few minutes to see what other thoughts it brings with it. If it does not bring any at first, do not let that disturb you, but wait a few minutes every time that you think of this, and see if any other passages come to you. Live with this passage of scripture for as long as possible: a day, a week, a month, pondering it as many times a day as you can bring yourself to remember it consciously. Then you will discover that your consciousness of this truth does build your house, and it is not built in vain.

Across the Desk

Long ago, Jesus said, "Ye are the light of the world." Followers of his teaching should surely think seriously about this statement for it shows us what our mission in the world is. To be the light of the world, we must let the light shine through us to illumine the world. That light is love, so we must let love shine through us; that light is truth, so we must be a beacon of truth.

Our work is to meditate until we feel the flow, feel that light within, and then release it into the world. This is our only reason for being here. This is fulfilling the divine plan.

Chapter Eight

Scripture As a Way of Life

All spiritual teaching reveals that we are meant to live, not "by bread alone, but by every word that proceedeth out of the mouth of God"[1] which, of course, means every word of God that we can receive, every word of God that we can hear. We are told that God is not in the whirlwind: God is in the "still small voice."[2] The power of God is not external to us; the power of God is within us; and the power of God must reveal itself within us and flow out from us.

If we are to have a contact with God and receive the word of God in us, it must be through our consciousness, and for this to happen, there must be built up in us a state of receptivity. We have been so conditioned that we can hear all the external noises; we can hear everything that is taking place outside of us, but we cannot hear that Word that is always imparting Itself within, until we develop an inner sense, a listening or receptive sense, until that still small voice can break through; and then through it, we receive the impartation of God by means of which we are to live.

In the years in which we are developing that spiritual aware-ness, we follow a practice of abiding in the word of truth until we arrive at a place where it is no longer an intellectual process, but an intuitive awareness within us. Scripture was given to us because a need was felt which resulted in the bibles of the world.

Early Methods of Revealing Scriptural Wisdom

In the early days when very few people could read or write, skills reserved only for the very few, the major portion of the writings that existed and were known to the people, except those which were related to the arts and sciences, was of a scriptural or religious nature.

Among scholars who lived in monasteries, it was possible to live without the written word because they had close contact with the word of scripture which was spoken and heard day in and day out, night in and night out. But part of their work was to preserve the ancient scriptures by copying them by hand and illuminating them with rare artistry. These handwritten manuscripts, containing the scriptural wisdom of the ages, were circulated among the relatively few who could read.

One of the greatest thrills of all my travels came to me in Damascus, where at the museum I saw an entire room which had been part of a Hebrew synagogue that existed about 200 A.D. and was found buried some several hundred miles from Damascus. When the building was unearthed, it was found possible to move the hand-painted walls and ceiling intact to Damascus and put them together as a room. Every one of the paintings in this room represents a Bible scene or tells a Bible story, and they were important for the spiritual enlightenment of the people of that day because there was no printed Bible at that time. There were only the handwritten manuscripts passed around the Holy Land. Yet these stories were exactly as they are given to us in scripture today, and the paintings are still beautifully preserved.

In spite of the fact that only a few had a knowledge of reading and writing, nevertheless wherever it was possible, these manuscripts were circulated, and pictures setting forth the stories of scripture were drawn that made these truths available to many more of the people than were able to read.

Why did men give their lives to this great labor of placing scripture before the people? It was because it was considered important that people learn to live, not alone by farming, by building, or doing anything else, but "by every word that proceedeth out of the mouth of God," and revealing the message of scripture through manuscripts and art was their way of teaching.

Is it not significant that the first book printed with movable type was the Bible? Does it not tell us the importance that learned, dedicated, and religious men placed on Scripture?

Aids to Bible Study

Hundreds and hundreds of millions of copies of the Bible have been circulated, but familiarity breeds contempt. We have become so accustomed to owning a Bible or finding one available for a dollar that on the whole most persons have lost their appreciation of the Bible—not that nearly everyone does not own one, but how few appreciate it enough to make a study of its message and to apply its principles! Yet, not only to own a Bible but to know how to study it is the way whereby we can learn to live by the word of God.

Because of this, scholars have gone to great lengths to prepare concordances to the Bible. With the use of a concordance, the whole Bible is opened to anyone who is searching, because there is not a subject or a quotation a person could want to look up in the Bible that he could not find. There is not a subject on which he could not build up for himself six, eight, or ten Bible passages to live with. Anyone would be surprised at the treasures that are in a Bible when he sits down with a concordance. If we take the word "protection," the word "care," the word "love," the word "life," or the word "prayer" and go through the concordance, we will see what the word of God can do once we have it embedded and embodied in our consciousness.

The kingdom of God is within, but it is overlaid with centuries of materialistic thinking and living which have brought about a sense of separation from God. It has not brought about a separation from God, only a *sense* of separation. Man and God are not separate. Jesus did not say that the kingdom of God was two hundred million light years away from us in a place called heaven. He said that the kingdom of God is within us. The kingdom of God is not up, and the kingdom of the devil is not down, but the kingdom of God is within us, and in our sense of separation, the kingdom of hell is within us also—not very far from us.

When we have that word of scripture in us and know that the kingdom of God is within us, we find ten million miles of space drop away from us. We will not then be looking outside ourselves and wondering how to contact God or how to bring God into our experience. We will relax with that one statement, "The kingdom of God is within you."[3] It is neither lo here nor lo there: it is within; and with that relaxing, almost instantaneously, an awareness takes over, and actual touch that comes to us from the Father within.

Turn and Live Through Scripture

> For I have no pleasure in the death
> of him that dieth, saith the Lord God:
> wherefore turn yourselves, and live ye.
> Ezekiel 18:32

If we search the scriptures, we will learn, not only from the great Hebrew prophets, but from Jesus, John, and Paul, that God has no pleasure in our dying; that if we turn from our materialistic ways, from the sinful way of life, we will live. It is the mission of the Christ to heal the sick, to raise the dead, to feed the hungry, and to forgive the sinner.

It is not the function of the Christ to condemn sinners to hell; it is not the function of the Christ to condemn sinners to limbo or any place else where ignorance has decreed that mankind should go; but rather the function of the Christ is to forgive sinners, and to heal them, not to judge, criticize, or condemn them. It is not true that God visits disease on His children or involves them in automobile accidents in order to bring them home to Him. A study of scripture will prove that none of this is true. If we abide in the word of God, the evils of the world will not come nigh our dwelling place, and we will bear fruit richly.

> He that dwelleth in the secret place of the most High
> shall abide under the shadow of the Almighty.
> Psalm 91:1

Evil becomes a part of our experience because we do not dwell in the secret place of the most High. We do not consciously abide in our oneness with God; we do not acknowledge that "except the Lord build the house, they labour in vain that build it."[4] Failure does not come because God wants to teach us a lesson; it does not come because we are being punished for something: failure comes only because we do not live, move, and have our being in the acknowledgment that we cannot build a house, we cannot build a business, we cannot build any permanent success except the Lord build it for us.

Since the Master said, "I can of mine own self do nothing,"[5] how much more should we realize that we cannot begin the day until we are armed with power from on High?

> I will not go out into this world until I have placed on
> me the armor of God, which is the word of God, or Truth.

As was pointed out in the July *Letter,* revealed truth is virtually the same in every scripture that is known to man. All the great principles that we find in the Hebrew testament are repeated in the Christian testament, and most of them are also to be found in Hindu and Chinese scripture. There is only one truth, and that truth has been revealed to men in every part of the globe who have been receptive and responsive to the word of God. When they received it, it was always the same word of God, because there is only one God. When God spoke to Abraham, Isaac, Jacob, or Moses, it could not have been a different God from the one that spoke to Jesus, John, or Paul; and if there is only one God, that same God must have spoken to Buddha and Lao-tse. There is only one God and there is only one truth, but people in different centuries and in different parts of the world heard that revealed truth, and the truth revealed to them became the scriptures as we know them today.

A famous theologian has said that it is not enough to read or talk about God but that every individual must have a God-experience, and that is possible. He further went on to say that God is not confined to Christianity, nor is God confined to the organized church, but that God is Spirit, available to all men, and is to be experienced by all men. That really takes God out of time and space and makes Him universally omnipresent wherever man can be: in any age, in any time, in any color. That, of course, is the essence of the message of the Infinite Way, because without this ability to receive the word of God in our consciousness, what possibility is there of our living in obedience to the teaching of the Master? If we cannot receive the word of God, if we cannot be led, guided, and directed by it, how can we live by it?

The barrier to our individual God-experience is, of course, an inbuilt egotism which has come to us, not by anyone's fault, but through centuries of living separate and apart from the actual experience of God, living out not from the experience itself, but merely on sermons or books. This is the reason that we have difficulty in opening ourselves to an inner receptivity to that "still small voice" which is within us and which is waiting to feed and clothe us, heal us, lift us up from the dead, wipe out all the years of the "locusts,"[6] and cleanse us of our sins of the past in the same way the Master did: "Neither do I condemn thee: go, and sin no more."[7] There was not to be a probationary period in hell in which to suffer hell's furies, but an immediate forgiveness, being forgiven and forgiving.

Love As an Act

You must remember that the greatest power on earth, in heaven, or in hell is the power of love; but love is not an emotion, and love is not a word. Love can never be expressed in words. Love is an act. As a matter of fact, the very words, "I love you," can be covering up the opposite. A spoken word of love has no more relationship to love than speaking the word God has any relationship to God. No one is ever going to know God by saying, "God," and no one is ever going to love by saying, "Love."

Love is an act, and it is not only an act, it is a series of acts. It must be love in action, which means care, thoughtfulness, forgiveness, consideration, cooperation, and benevolence. It was expressed by Paul in that same way when he said that of all the things that are important, the greatest is love. Yes, the greatest is love; but not the word "love," the act of love.

How do we know this from scripture? The Master said very little about love, except to admonish us to love the Lord with all our heart and to love our neighbor as ourselves; but he said a great deal about love in action when he spoke of forgiveness, when he taught the importance of feeding the hungry, healing the sick, visiting the prisoner in prison, consoling the mourner. None of this had anything to do with speech: this all had to do with action.

For I was an hungred, and ye gave me meat:
I was thirsty, and ye gave me drink:
I was a stranger, and ye took me in:

Naked, and ye clothed me: I was sick, and ye visited
me: I was in prison, and ye came unto me.
Matthew 25:35, 36

If we look at the life of Jesus, we will see that when the woman sinned, he forgave her; when the multitudes were hungry, he fed them; when Lazarus was dead, he raised him up; and all this had nothing to do with words. It all had to do with acts.

Metaphysicians have foolishly believed that when they think, declare, or read prayers, affirmations, or treatments, there will be an answer from God. But there is no answer from God except in the fulfillment of the laws of God. It is not enough to sit back and desire that we be healed. It is not sufficient that we sit back and desire that the Lord God come down out of His holy temple and provide for us. It is not going to happen that way.

As we open ourselves to the vision and the realization of God, we have to *act* as if we were children of God and put into operation the laws of God. "Thou shalt love the Lord thy God with all thy heart, and with all thy soul, and with all thy mind. . . . Thou shalt love thy neighbour as thyself."[8] These words are not prayers: they are commands, and when those commands are obeyed, fulfillment takes place. Prayer is an activity: it is the activity of the soul, the mind, and the body. All three have to work together in fulfilling the commandments.

"The Fast That I Have Chosen"

The Hebrew fasts from sunup to sundown. As a matter of fact, that is a good idea, more especially if it is done in the way that is required in the old orthodox temple: to go to the temple in the morning and stay there all day, fasting, praying, cogitating, asking forgiveness for sins. By the time a person leaves the temple in the evening, all his sins are supposed to have been forgiven, and he begins with a clean slate—but not a clean slate to go out tomorrow and start all over again. That is not really prayer, that is not atonement, and that is not fasting.

But if on a certain day, you and I come to the realization that our life has not been lived up to the highest expression of what we know of love, and we would like to start out from a higher basis, then we can come to a day of fasting, a day of prayer, or it can be a day of feasting. As long as within us there is the realization, "I have come to the end of an era. I have come to the end of an episode; I have come to the end of this particular phase of my life, and I'm starting afresh," we have fasted. We have repented; we are abstaining from those old ways; and now we are beginning anew. In that day, we have had our day of atonement and have been forgiven.

Isaiah made it very clear that fasting, praying, afflicting our soul, or asceticism of any kind is nothing—nothing if it is done for any reason other than one.

> Is not this the fast that I have chosen? to loose the bands
> of wickedness, to undo the heavy burdens, and to let the
> oppressed go free, and that ye break every yoke?
>
> Is it not to deal thy bread to the hungry, and that
> thou bring the poor that are cast out to thy house?
> when thou seest the naked, that thou cover him;
> and that thou hide not thyself from thine own flesh?
>
> Then shall thy light break forth as the morning,
> and thine health shall spring forth speedily:
> and thy righteousness shall go before thee;
> the glory of the Lord shall be thy reward.

> And if thou draw out thy soul to the hungry, and sat-
> isfy the afflicted soul; then shall thy light rise in
> obscurity, and thy darkness be as the noon day:
>
> And the Lord shall guide thee continually, and satisfy
> thy soul in drought, and make fat thy bones: and
> thou shalt be like a watered garden, and like a spring
> of water, whose waters fail not.
> Isaiah 58:6-8, 10, 11

That is loving thy neighbor as thyself. That is living the life of prayer.

The major function of the Infinite Way is to reveal, through discernment of scripture, a spiritual way of life, and then help those who desire it to attain it. They cannot attain it of their own accord. Somebody must introduce to them the spiritual activity of the Christ that will enable them to attain, for no man by his own power can attain: there must be the activity of a spiritual awareness within. That is brought to us either by a teacher, practitioner, books, scripture, or whatever it is that lifts us in consciousness to the point of inner receptivity to the Christ.

Loving God Supremely

Let us live prayer and put into action the commandment to love God with all our heart. This means to acknowledge God as the infinite, invisible, creative Principle of the universe, and to acknowledge that to God there is no opposite, no opposition. Because of this truth, we need no power.

In being confronted with any problem, whether our own or another's, let us have no resistance in our mind, no desire to refute, to deny, to overcome, to rise above, or to destroy—just that calm peace. Because we have acknowledged God as the only creative, maintaining, and sustaining Principle, we know there is no other power, so we need not invoke any power for any purpose.

When we are in meditation and are not struggling with a problem, we are not then trying to overcome it, destroy it, or rise above it. If necessary, we are looking right at it and not even needing God, since we know that God already is. Then we are loving God with all our heart, because we are giving It utter supremacy and not acknowledging that there is something we want It to do something to.

Loving Our Neighbors on Their Level

As for loving our neighbor, does not Isaiah show that unless we are meeting the need of our brother at his level of consciousness, we are neglecting part of that loving? Our neighbors are not all metaphysicians. It is true that we need not take pity on our spiritual brother and sister; we need not support them, because the greatest thing we have of value to them in the way of love is, "Look, brother and sister, let us not rely on human modes or means. Let us stand fast in spiritual demonstration and see what the Lord your God hath for you." That is the highest form of loving our neighbor that we can give to our spiritual brother and sister.

But we have other neighbors, neighbors who may need a hospital. Let us help to give it to them. We have neighbors who still need certain schools. We have neighbors who need food and some who need clothing. Let us be a neighbor on *their* level, and that does not mean that we acknowledge that that is absolutely necessary. We acknowledge that it is necessary only at their level of consciousness, and they are our neighbors too. We cannot say to them, "You starve to death until you get our understanding." The Master fed the multitudes and he healed them. He did not say to them, "I won't help you until you are as spiritual as I am," but he fed them at their level of consciousness. And so should we.

We have to put love into action. Prayers are not words or thoughts. Words and thoughts may be a part of prayer to a certain point, but beyond that point, prayer is action. As we reach a certain level of spiritual consciousness, we are given certain spiritual tasks to do even on what we call this human plane, and it behooves us to do those things.

Scripture Must Become an Act

In scripture, we learn that Jesus gave no sermon when his disciple cut the ear off one of the soldiers. He did not sermonize; he merely made a statement: "Put up again thy sword into his place,"[9]—an action! And he explained why, "for all they that take the sword shall perish with the sword."[9] Very short and very sweet! But trying to live up to that one statement would take a whole lifetime.

If we are studying scripture—not reading it, not rushing through it, not mumbling it to ourselves—and we come to a passage such as, "Resist not evil," following that, too, is an act. If anyone thinks that it is not hard, let him try to resist not evil, and he will see what a difficult act it is. How many months it would take to live those few words, to be able to put them into demonstrable action! But when we have succeeded, we would find the effect those words would have on our life, because the only way we can arrive at the state of consciousness that resists not evil is to come to the realization of these scriptural passages:

> Thou couldest have no power at all against me,
> except it were given thee from above.
> John 19:11

> Be strong and courageous, be not afraid nor
> dismayed for the king of Assyria. . . .

> With him is an arm of flesh; but with us is the Lord
> our God to help us, and to fight our battles.
>   II Chronicles 32:7,8

What a revelation of God's allness! But that realization does not come unless, first of all, we know these passages of scripture and specifically practice them until they become a way of life. Then we are living the Christian way of life. As long as we are merely declaring these statements or hearing them in a lecture, class, or sermon, we are not living Christianity. We live Christianity only when we begin to assimilate these passages of scripture and then try to measure each day to see how much we have succeeded or failed to live up to them.

At first it is discouraging to discover that we may be living the Christian way of life only about one-tenth of one percent, but it is a beautiful way of life by the time we get to the place where we can say, "Why, I think today I made one percent in my examination. I only missed by ninety-nine percent."And that is a good day, a very good day. But I will tell you the truth: we do have days when we get up to two or three percent. Just think what we have to look forward to: staying here on earth until we get up to around seventy, eighty, or ninety percent. That will give us a good long life on earth, and a useful one.

New Meanings Through
Spiritual Discernment of the Bible

There are books that are helpful to a student of the Bible, although most of them are a little bit too simple for our students because they make it too easy to become just affirmers of quotations. They are sometimes helpful to turn to, however, because in moments when we do not have time to look in the concordance to find some passage for us, we can turn to such a book as *The Runner's Bible* or some other book that has Bible texts,

and quickly find a passage that we can take into our consciousness and live with. But let us not let the use of those books cheat
us of the opportunity of working with concordances, because
with a concordance, we will find things that we never knew
were in the Bible, things that open up whole trends of thought,
new vistas of consciousness.

Sometimes I come half into agreement with some of those
religious sects that forbid their families to read anything except
the Bible, maintaining that all other books are unnecessary. Of
course, we cannot go all the way with them on that. Actually,
however, if there is a choice, the Bible is the best of books, if it can
be taken as a way of life and not just read in order to be able to
say sanctimoniously, "I read the Bible from cover to cover once a
year." There is no profit in that, a little glory, but no profit. The
profit that comes from reading the Bible is in being able to select
a passage of Scripture, take it into meditation, ponder it, try to get
back into the spirit and experience of the one who revealed it, or
the circumstances that brought it forth, and then seeing whole
new meanings that are brought to light by those things.

For example, as we read of Moses and the opening of the
Red Sea, of the manna falling from the sky, and of the protection that Moses had in the forty years of going across the desert,
and inwardly ponder the meaning and essence of these experiences, eventually comes the understanding that the Spirit was
traveling with that man, performing these things. It was not the
man; he was armed with the power of God. It was the power of
God that had come to conscious awakening in him that performed this thing. The other Hebrews had not had the experience on the Mount that he had had, that awakening, that light,
that revelation of the name and nature of God. Man, inspired
and empowered with the spirit of God, is quite a different thing
from a man who is a shepherd on the hills.

When we watch Elijah going through his troubles after he
had been chased out into the wilderness, we find that one day

when he was hungry, he was fed by a poor widow who had little or nothing herself. Another day, ravens brought him food; another day, he found cakes baked on the stones in front of him; and we ask ourselves: Is this true? Is this possible? Yes, it is, and if we keep our mind open and listen, it is revealed to us that it is true. It would not have been true if Elijah had been there alone, but there was a Spirit in Elijah which spoke to him and finally said, "I have left me seven thousand in Israel, all the knees which have not bowed unto Baal."[10]

The Miracles of God-Awareness

As we study scripture and encompass centuries and centuries of life in the Holy Land, an unbelievable awakening comes when we begin to perceive, as recounted in Isaiah, that long before the days of the Master, there was a man who foresaw the whole three-year ministry of the Master: spoke of it, quoted it line for line, and told everything that would happen during his time on earth. We might ask: Was this man a fortuneteller? No, the spirit of God inspired him and revealed all things unto him, so that he knew the past, the present, and the future, and he knew the penalties that would come to those who would not listen to the still small voice—not a penalty from God, a penalty a person brings upon himself.

Then, if we skip over a few centuries and come to Christ Jesus and follow his three years of ministry, there is recounted one miracle after another. Reading these passages over and over again, the first thing we realize is that we are reading the story of an ordained Hebrew rabbi, a man who preached in the Hebrew synagogues. Just a Hebrew rabbi! Then all of a sudden we smile. Just a Hebrew rabbi? Oh, no, this is a different one! There were no other Hebrew rabbis like this one! What set this one apart? It was because in all these miracles there was a Spirit working in that man. He was able to say, "I can of mine own self do nothing.[11]. . . The Father that dwelleth in me, he doeth the works."[12] Here is a God-conscious man, a man with God-awareness, a man who knew that there was the Spirit dwelling in him. Then we say, "Well, no wonder the miracles took place. They took place by the grace of God."

Forty or fifty years later in the New Testament, we come to Paul, a Hebrew teacher in a synagogue, just a man, a tent-maker. Then we begin to read of his miracles and his power with men. Again we ask, "Is this a man?" And we look back and real-ize, "Why, no, on the road to Damascus, something happened to that man, and he was not just a man any more. Now he is a man who does not merely have the letter of the Hebrew scrip-ture. He is a man imbued and inspired with the Spirit."

Saul was one of the most learned of men in Hebrew scrip-ture, but what good was that to him? He could not have healed a headache with it; but on a certain day, scripture came alive in him. The Light broke through. Now Saul is not Saul anymore, but Paul: a missionary, a follower of the Christ, a teacher of the Christ. Twenty centuries later he lives in the minds of men when many of the disciples who actually walked with the Master are scarcely remembered, except by their names, but cer-tainly not by their deeds. Paul is remembered, not for his name, but for his deeds. Few even remember that Paul at one time was known as Saul.

Whence came those deeds? From that moment of inspira-tion, that moment of illumination, that moment when the words of scripture were not a dead ritual to be read on Saturday and on feast and fast days, but when they were to be taken into life every day of the week, seven days a week, lived and put into action!

It was Paul who really began the Christian era. Up to his time, all the Master's teaching was confined to the Hebrew faith and to Hebrews, as if all this good were to be restricted to one people and one religion. Paul broke through that, and Paul revealed that the Christ-teaching is not a teaching for a man, a race, a creed, or a religion; it is a teaching for the world; it is to be lived! It is not meant only for Saturdays or Sundays; it is not only for holidays and holy days; this is to be lived; and every day we are to put love into action.

Changes Brought About by the Word Entertained in Consciousness

Is it not clear that the chances of any person's ever having a Moses-experience, an Elijah-experience, an Isaiah-experience, a Jesus-experience, or a Paul-experience are very small except in proportion as scripture is alive in him? These men were all men burning up inside with scripture, with the word of God. I have never heard of an individual who became spiritually great who was not versed in scripture and who was not making of scripture a life. Our evangelists of today are men who live by scripture, and through their living with scripture, some spark opens in them. The word of God becomes alive. It is not dead print on a page any more: it is in electric lights, neon lights.

A person's life changes. In the past thirty years I have watched hundreds of people who have come out of ordinary life, with no more knowledge of scripture than they were able to pick up by attending a church service or something of that kind, and after they began to live with scripture and to make the passages of scripture a part of their everyday living, I have seen the change in their nature, in their character, in their lives, in their health, and in their supply. I have watched a complete change in human relationships the very moment that scripture became a living word to them. That is why every message that is in the Infinite Way writings is a message based on some passage of scripture, some incident or some story of scripture, but brought alive by the inspiration and the revelation that have been given to me on the subject.

If the passages of scripture quoted in my writings were lift-ed out of them, we would have enough without anything else, because the words of scripture will never pass away. They are the word of Truth, found in all scripture: the Hebrew, the Christian, the Oriental, the Moslem. There we find all these passages that make men live, and live by the word of God.

When we study and search the scriptures, we are fed as we never before have been fed; we are guided, directed, protected as we never before have been; but always in direct proportion as we make these passages of scripture our daily bread.

Sometimes when I tell classes that we must not pray to God for things, some people will come back and say to me, "Oh, but Jesus said, 'Give us this day our daily bread.' "[13] Such persons have not studied scripture. All they have learned to do is to read it with-out knowing its meaning, because the Master was very clear that we are not to ask for bread, we are not to ask for what we shall eat, or what we shall drink, or wherewithal we shall be clothed.

Then what did he mean when he prayed: "Give us this day our daily bread"? Did he not later reveal, "I am the bread of life."[14] And does not John tell us, "And the Word was made flesh."[15] Ah, then our prayer is: give us this Word, give us this bread, this wine, this water, this meat that *I* am; the word of God, the word of Truth.

As we pray daily that the word of God be given to us and as we take that Word in the form of scriptural passages into our daily living, what a difference takes place in our entire experi-ence in just a few months!

Regardless of the lions that we face on the street, the storms, or the headlines, let us not forget that God is not in these; power is not in these: all power is in the still small voice within us. God is not in the problems, God is not in the storms of life, God is not external to us; God is in the still, small voice within us. There is no power in the storm; there is no power in the external circum-stance: all the power there is, is in the still, small voice within.

Across the Desk

In this *Letter,* Joel writes of the importance of using a concordance to the Bible. You have already been doing this if you followed the suggestion in March to look up references on light. Those who did have surely found that this work was helpful in making that transition from a material state of consciousness to spiritual awareness.

If you have not followed through on other words, some of which are suggested in this month's *Letter,* by all means do so. To meditate on some of these passages that you will find in the Bible will bring to your awareness the wisdom of some of the great spiritual lights of all time. Then live with these gems throughout the day until they become your very own consciousness.

Chapter Nine

I Have

In the mean while his disciples prayed him,
saying, Master, eat.

But he said unto them,
I have meat to eat that ye know not of.

John 4:31,32

This passage of scripture has meant much to me, not only in my personal life, but in the unfoldment of the entire message of the Infinite Way. It is one that I share freely with the students because it illustrates an important spiritual principle. When contemplated and eventually understood, this passage is sufficient to lift anyone out of a mortal sense of life into divine consciousness; it is sufficient to change the entire nature of one's life on earth, to transform lack into abundance and sickness into health.

To human sense, everyone lacks something, and everyone is aware of that lack. Surprisingly enough, the little bit a person lacks is as nothing compared with what he already has, and yet instead of abiding in the awareness of what he already has, he takes that for granted, magnifying and multiplying what he has not by letting it occupy his thought, attention, and prayers.

When he turns from the little that he has and begins to ponder the abundance of what he has, he discovers many miracles of Grace. The first one that pops into his thought is: "I have life. It is really comforting to know that. Life is God, and if I have life, I have God. If I have God, what more could I want?"

It has been said that if a person had God and everything else in the world, he would have nothing more than if he had only God. God is infinite; God is all-inclusive; God embodies all there is. When one discovers that he has God, he also discovers that he has no other needs. To have the understanding that God constitutes one's very life brings with it the conviction that he is already eternal and immortal.

If a person abides in the truth that he has meat the world knows not of, that he has that water, wine, and bread of life, he soon discovers that he has everything needful for his unfoldment without taking thought for his life.

> I have meat; my consciousness is this meat, my Self is
> this meat. I embody within my consciousness,
> within my Self, the infinite allness of God.
> Right now I am in God, and God is in me.
> I am abiding in the allness of God, and the allness
> of God is abiding in me. I am one with the infinite
> source of life, truth, and love. I am one with the
> infinite storehouse of this entire universe.

"Such As I Have Give I Thee"

Truth made active in your consciousness becomes the invisible source, substance, and activity of your outer experience. But it does more than that. In the degree that you can maintain this spiritual atmosphere, even if for brief moments of the day and night, persons everywhere reaching out to God's grace will receive blessings through you of which you will never be aware. Think what can happen in the experience of those persons around the world who attune themselves to the united consciousness of a group of students wholly and completely dedicated to Infinite Way principles and to nothing else. Think of the spiritual truths they touch! Think of the spiritual love with which they are enfolded!

At some time or other, almost everyone who has sought Truth, or God, was probably seeking healing: physical, mental, moral, or financial. Even while he thought he was seeking these healings, however, he really was seeking God, he was seeking Truth, and he had the right to expect that those to whom he went for help in his search had found some measure of the realization of God. He had the right, though he did not know it then, to expect that those to whom he went were maintaining themselves in a consciousness of Truth. In other words, he had the right to expect of his practitioner or teacher a spiritual integrity. When he went to the consciousness of a teacher, he had the right to find spiritual truth in the teacher's consciousness, and to find him living in spiritual truth, because a teacher has nothing to give but that.

Peter said, "Silver and gold have I none; but such as I have give I thee."[1] What is it that John and Peter had that day at the Temple Gate Beautiful? Silver and gold they had none; place and position in life they had none. All that they had was their spiritual integrity, that is, their abiding in the word of God and their letting the word of God abide in them. They had a consciousness that was to some extent lifted above earthly things, a consciousness in which they were maintaining Truth, and in which Truth was maintaining them. Then, because the crippled beggar entered that consciousness of Truth, he was enabled to leap up dancing, healed.

The Blessings of an
Uplifted Consciousness

Whenever you have gone to a practitioner or a teacher who was maintaining himself in the Spirit, you received healing: physical, mental, moral, or financial. In the degree that these practitioners or teachers were lifted above the things of the earth, they could lift you up into some measure of spiritual realization, into some measure of attained spiritual consciousness.

You do not always have the power to lift yourself, but you can be lifted by those who have gone a step beyond you. That is why it is written, "I, if I be lifted up from the earth, will draw all men unto me."[2] But there is that "if": "I, if I be lifted up." If the practitioner or teacher is not lifted up in consciousness, if he is not abiding in the Word and the Word is not abiding in him, he cannot lift other men up to spiritual consciousness. But if you find him in the Spirit, if you find him abiding in Truth, in the divine consciousness, if you come to him when he is lifted up above the discords and inharmonies of the earth, you in turn are lifted up.

At first you may only be lifted up to the point of being healed of some discord, but eventually, when you yourself are sufficiently freed of earth-ties, then you can be lifted up by the practitioner's or teacher's state of consciousness into the divine, into the spiritual. Every person thinking of himself as a practitioner or teacher or any person thinking of himself as being on the spiritual path has a real responsibility, and that is to maintain himself in a high state of consciousness.

There are many ways of doing this. It can be done through the reading or the hearing of the spiritual word. You can attain it by your meditations; you can attain it in that atmosphere where two or more are gathered together in spiritual oneness; you can attain it when there are "ten righteous men"[3] meeting together. You maintain yourself spiritually by not reacting to the appearances in the world and by not permitting yourself to be dragged down by them.

Ask yourself what people are going to meet when they enter your spiritual household. Whenever Infinite Way students meet together, they are "the two or three gathered together in my name,"[4] they are the "ten righteous men" in a city. The question is: Do you recognize your responsibility to other Infinite Way students all over the globe? Being faithful to that responsibility, you are not only a blessing to Infinite Way students, but to anyone and everyone who may be reaching out to God, because in reaching out to God, whether or not a person knows it, he is reaching out to the God-consciousness of those individuals who live in that state of consciousness.

Your Responsibility to the Stranger

There is no divine consciousness floating around in the air. The divine consciousness is made manifest as the consciousness of an individual or as a world of individuals. The woman who broke through the throng to touch the hem of the Robe did not break through the throng to touch just anybody's robe. It was the Master's robe she wanted to touch. Why the Master out of all that throng? Because he was the one in whom and through whom the divine consciousness was reaching the earth. Therefore, divine consciousness, functioning as his individual consciousness, was available to anyone who reached out to touch It.

People all over the world who are reaching out to God are never going to find God somewhere out in space. Unless they find God as the consciousness of individual being, they are not going to find God at all. Therefore, everyone who knows this truth has a responsibility, and that responsibility is for you to decide what a stranger will find when he enters your consciousness. What does a person in prison or a person in a hospital find when he reaches out to God? A blank space with no answer? Or can he find your consciousness and find that you are a transparency through which God can reach him?

Everywhere people are reaching out for safety, for security, for peace on earth, for healing. They do not realize that these things cannot be attained or achieved unless they touch the consciousness of someone who is abiding in the Word and letting the Word abide in him. There is no peace except the peace that the Hebrews found through Moses, that the Christians found through Jesus, that the Buddhists found through Buddha. There must be individual consciousness attuned to God; there must be individual consciousness setting aside some periods of the day to forget personal problems, family problems, and the nation's problems, in order that individual consciousness may rise above the earth-plane into a state of divine Consciousness whereby it becomes a transparency through which God reaches the earth.

Establish Yourself in the Consciousness of Truth and Love

In participating in an Infinite Way meeting, your responsibility is to check all your troubles at the door before you go in. Check your human responsibilities; check your human pains; check all those things that concern you. Leave them outside, and when you go into the room, wherever that may be, attune yourself to God. Spend your hour forgetting your own problems and in attunement with God. Abide in some word of God, and let the word of God abide in you. Contemplate some passage of truth. If you are lost in the contemplation of some spiritual truth, you will lose nothing, even if you do not hear a word that is spoken from the platform.

As you abide in this truth, everyone around the globe

who is reaching out to the united consciousness of an Infinite Way class is coming into a consciousness of life eternal, a consciousness of spiritual truth and love—not human affection. That is there, too, but it does not bless anyone except the few individuals who share in that human affection. You are filled with the spirit of divine Love because of this recognition:

> My consciousness is filled
> with the love of God.
> I have the wine of inspiration
> abiding with me, and all those who
> touch my consciousness are not now aware
> of a human being: they are aware of this
> consciousness that is filled with truth and love.

Because you and all those who are a part of an Infinite Way meeting are abiding in the Word, you are the two or more gathered together: you are the ten righteous men; and therefore you are a united consciousness.

Numbers are of no importance. It really makes no difference if there are two of you, ten or a thousand. Numbers do not increase the degree of spirituality. What determines the degree of spirituality is a unitedness in spiritual truth. So if only two are abiding in spiritual truth, they are that two gathered together, and if there were a thousand and a united thousand, there would still be that oneness, and the presence of the thousand would not increase it. It is the measure of the oneness that determines the degree of spirituality.

When your consciousness is a consciousness filled with the allness of God, think what is happening to every individual who is now attuned to that consciousness: your friends, your relatives, or the stranger. Think of what is happening to them as they touch your consciousness of abundance, your consciousness of life, your consciousness of love!

Becoming the Light of the World

Just as you, at any time in the twenty-four hours of the day, may have some need, some problem, or some claim which causes you to reach out to the divine Consciousness, and just as you would like to feel or know that somewhere around the globe there is at least one individual attuned to God and that your reaching out to God attunes you to that individual, so your responsibility throughout the day and throughout the night is to remember that somewhere on earth there are those reaching out to God, and the only hope there is of their reaching God is in their reaching individual consciousness attuned to God. There is, therefore, a responsibility on your shoulders to maintain yourself in God-consciousness, realizing that since God-consciousness and your individual consciousness are one, you as an individual are the transparency through which that divine consciousness is reaching the earth.

As you abide in that many times a day, and a few times at night, you become the light of the world. In the beginning when this is first pointed out to you, it may be true that, because of the necessity of human living and its pull, you will not remember this twenty-four hours a day, but there will be many times in the day when you will be pulled up sharply and reminded that you have allowed yourself to get mesmerized by the things of this earth, and then for a moment or two you pause to lift yourself above it, and in those moments somebody receives a blessing.

As time goes on, you become less and less mesmerized by the earth's pull. You remain in the world, but not of it. You continue to do your particular job, whether in the home, in business, in a profession, or whatever it may be, but you find that you are developing an area of consciousness that never comes down to earth. There is one little bit of you that never again gets involved in the things of this world. All the other part of you may have problems; all the other part of you may be working out of things; but that one little place in your consciousness is reserved and is always singing the song: "All that the Father has is mine. The place whereon I stand is holy ground. I am a transparency through which divine Grace reaches the earth. I am in the presence of my Father, and the Father is within me." It is this area of consciousness that the people of the world contact, and because of this, they find some measure of freedom from their problems.

Maintaining a Consciousness of Truth Is a Now-Activity

Every human being is hypnotized into accepting appearances as reality. It is only as a person learns to abide in the Word that he becomes less human and more divine and eventually is able to subordinate his humanness and live more and more and more in the divinity of his being.

No one can yet claim that he is abiding twenty-four hours of every day in the full and complete realization of his spiritual identity, but forgetting most of the earth's problems of the past and even of the present, he can look forward to a greater attainment of spiritual awareness than he has now. It never will be attained, however, except in proportion to what takes place in his consciousness now. The spiritualizing of consciousness cannot be put off until an hour from now. That has to be done in this instant.

When you are busy about your own affairs and this awareness has dropped from your conscious thinking and all of a sudden it comes back, you cannot say, "Ah, tonight I will spend an hour in divine consciousness." No, the moment that push comes, regardless of what else you are doing, regardless of what your body or your mind is doing, somewhere in your consciousness there must be a return to this realization: "I and the Father are one; therefore, I have meat." Then you are ready to go on about your work again. You have fulfilled yourself.

It takes only a few seconds of anyone's time to return to the Father's house. This is not accomplished in time or space; it is not anything that takes a long time. It takes only the willingness to remember any moment of now this truth:

I have meat. Silver and gold I may have none,
but I have meat, and wine, and water, and bread.
I have the spiritual staff of life. In fact,
all that the Father has is mine: all of the Spirit,
all of spiritual truth, all of spiritual reality.

The First Step, the Opening of Consciousness

Your consciousness is the avenue through which everything happens to you, through you, or by you. If you do not open your consciousness to a thing, it cannot happen. You yourself may not consciously know how you came to a spiritual teaching, but I am telling you that within you, your consciousness was opened to truth. No one will ever open a Bible or a book of truth unless first his consciousness has awakened to its need for the Bible or for a message of truth.

God can never enter your consciousness until your consciousness acknowledges a need for God. Something takes place within your Self. And what is the Self if not consciousness? Something took place within your consciousness that opened you to something or somebody. The woman who went through the throng recognized that the Master was a transparency for God. Peter recognized that the Master was the Christ, a transparency for the activity of God. Always there must be some recognition, "I know thee who thou art."[5] Consciousness must open and say, "I need God; I must have God; I want Truth." Then all the rest takes place in the outer realm.

Even without your knowing what you require, the moment

you are opened to the need for truth or want it, the right book is placed in your hands. Someone gives it to you; someone leaves it on a bus seat; or you are led to a library shelf. In one way or another, the moment your consciousness is opened to truth, truth has a way of finding entrance into your consciousness. In the beginning, you are aware of a lack: a lack of truth, a lack of God, a lack of life, a lack of health, or a lack of supply. By opening your consciousness, you make a way for truth to reach you, and eventually you learn a great secret: you learn that you always had God, you always had truth, you always had life eternal, you always had infinite substance, infinite supply, but your consciousness had been closed to it.

You may deny that your consciousness was not open to supply because you will say, "My consciousness has always been open to receive money." Ah, but money is not supply. The consciousness that is open to money is closed to supply. The consciousness that thought it was open to receiving good was really closed to receiving good, because consciousness is open to the supply of good only when it is open to the Spirit, for the Spirit is the only supply there is. Money and other material forms are merely the outer expression of an invisible substance.

Open Your Consciousness to the Bread, Meat, Wine, and Water

You may remember the story of the Hindu master who sent his disciple out for a piece of fruit, and had him cut open the fruit, asking what was in it. "A seed," was the response.

"Well, now, cut open the seed and see what is in it."

"The disciple cut open the seed and said, "Nothing. Nothing is in it."

The master answered, "It cannot be. It cannot be because out of nothing there could not come a seed, a tree, and fruit. There has to be something in that seed. It is there, but you cannot see it. It is life; it is God. That is what is at the center, the invisible center of all that is, for everything that is made was made of the substance of things which are not seen."

Invisible to your eyesight is the substance of which money, securities, and properties are formed, but be assured that money cannot make itself, securities cannot make themselves, properties cannot make themselves, nor can they deliver themselves to your door. It is the activity of an invisible something in your consciousness, and that something is Truth.

Everything that takes place in your life is going to take place as an activity of your consciousness. By an activity of your consciousness, by knowing the truth that God is the mind and the intelligence of this universe, even accidents can be prevented from taking place in your life. Because of omnipresence, this means that God is the divine intelligence universally; and therefore, intelligence and love are expressed everywhere at all times.

Present where you are is God, but if you do not open your consciousness to admit God, It can never be the bread, wine, and water, the activity of resurrection, that which restores to you "the years that the locust hath eaten."[6] It can be that to your neighbor, but not to you. You have to open your individual consciousness and acknowledge that you are the temple of God, that your body is the temple of God, that your consciousness is the temple of God.

> Within me is the presence of God, and the
> presence of God is the health of my countenance.
> There can be no health in my body if there is not
> an invisible presence of God which makes Itself
> manifest as this form and which is the harmony
> of this form. There can be no supply in my life if
> there is not an invisible Substance, an invisible
> Life at the center of my being which is the
> substance of my supply.

If you do not open your consciousness to this truth and abide in the Word and let the Word abide in you, the Presence that is within you is not functioning. Your own consciousness is the source, the center of your life. What you admit in consciousness, that you manifest in the outer.

> I have meat the world knows not of. I have a spring of living water within me. The bread of life, the wine of life, the water of life, the meat of life, and even the power of resurrection abide within my consciousness.

> Right here where I am is holy ground, for I am the temple of the living God. I am that place where God shines through. God is that invisible activity which appears outwardly as my health; God is the invisible substance and activity of my supply; God is even the invisible cement of my relationships: in my family, in business, and in my profession. My consciousness embodies the very spirit of God, the presence of God, the love of God, the life of God.

Establishing a New Pattern

The pattern of your outer life can be changed only by changing the pattern of your inner life. You first must have a pattern upon which your life is built, and that pattern is built in your consciousness, and the truths that you know become the harmonies that you manifest. Take the great truth, "I have meat the world knows not of," and secretly and sacredly hide that in Egypt, in the deepest, darkest recesses of your consciousness. Keep it as a precious seed, and by remembering and acknowledging it often, give it its water, its fertilizer, whatever it needs for its nourishment, by consciously remembering over and over:

I have meat; I have meat the world knows not of. I
need not look to man for my good. I and the Father
are one and all that the Father has is mine by the will
of God. No man can separate me from this: neither
life nor death can separate me from the care of God,
neither life nor death can separate me from God's
life, God's love, God's abundance, nor can any
human circumstance, for I and the Father are one,
not two. God's good does not have to reach me:
it is embodied in me, because of oneness.

The Hidden Meat

Every day when you become aware of some need in your
experience, turn, without any fear or doubt, and instantly
remember that you have the Christ, the spiritual substance of
life eternal, which will appear externally as that which satisfies
every need of the moment. If you are physically, mentally,
morally, or financially ill, accept this gift of God, and secretly
and sacredly, to yourself remember:

Thank you, Father, I have meat the world knows not
of: I have a hidden companionship; I have a hidden
source of supply; I have a hidden source of wisdom
and judgment; I have a hidden source of ideas.

Regardless of what it is that I may ever need in the
external world, hidden within me is the substance of
its form. Home, family, supply, companionship, joy,
peace, health, freedom, safety, security—
I have the substance of these, the essence of which
they are formed. Understanding this,
I can relax from fears and doubts, I can relax from
anxiety by abiding in this word of scripture.

> I will never hunger and thirst because I have this
> hidden meat, this hidden manna, this hidden sub-
> stance of all form. Except my home, my supply, or my
> business is fed by this hidden meat, it cannot endure.

If you will accept the meat that *I* give you, if you will accept the water that *I* give you, you will never hunger and you will never thirst, for the meat that *I* give you is this hidden meat, the meat the world knows not of.

Except the Lord build the house, except the Lord feed the house, it cannot endure. Do you see why? It is not the outer union of people or of governments; it is not through associations or contracts that you will find strength. Laws enacted by legislatures have been broken; contracts have been broken; agreements between nations have been broken. Human relationships, even that of parent and child, have been broken; but when the Lord builds the house, they labour in vain that try to destroy it.

> The meat that *I* give you, the wine and the water
> that *I* give you no man can take from you, because it
> is invisible: it is Truth within you. No one can take
> Truth from you, and the Truth is that which *I* am.
> Therefore, Truth is the bread, the meat, the wine,
> and the water. As long as you have this Truth,
> as long as you accept this meat that *I* offer you,
> and wine and water, you will never hunger,
> you will never thirst, you will never lack,
> you will never fail. There is no such thing as failure
> in the kingdom of God. There is no such thing
> as failure in a life that is built on My word.

Your strength is in the hidden meat, and this no enemies can reach. Their eyes cannot penetrate to the Invisible; there-fore, this meat can never be touched, destroyed, harmed, nor the temple which you are.

Regardless of whom you may believe your enemies to be or what they may be, do not depend on visible strength to over-come them. Do not depend on your muscles or your weapons; and even though your nation builds storehouses of arms, let your reliance be, not on those arms, but on the meat that *I* within give you, on the strength, on the inspiration.

> Father, You have offered me the hidden manna of
> Yourself, of Your kingdom within me. You have
> offered me infinite, eternal meat, wine, and water,
> and I accept. From this moment on, I will live
> secretly, silently, sacredly in the assurance that You
> have given me that meat which is Christ, that meat
> which is Spirit, that meat which is the spiritual
> substance of all form. I accept that as an invisible
> Substance that " man, whose breath is in his nostrils" [7]
> cannot see, cannot fight, and cannot reach.
> This life of mine is invisible, incorporeal. The temple
> which I am is invisible and incorporeal. It cannot be
> drowned with water; it cannot be burned with fire;
> it cannot be destroyed by bullets, nor can my
> substance be taken from me—my supply, my home,
> my family—for this is the meat the Father has given
> me. This is the divine union of I and my Father, and
> in this union, all that the Father has is mine.

The Father says, "Son, thou art ever with me, and all that I have is thine." [8] What does the Father have? Meat, wine, water, life, life everlasting, life eternal. "I am come that they might have life, and that they might have it more abundantly." [9] What sustains this life? The meat that the Father gives you.

Your values now are changed. You are not counting the dollars in your bank; you are not counting the investments in your vault or your properties; you are not counting on how many bombs the government stores up. You have made a transition in this moment to the spiritual life in which you are the temple of God. You are invisible, spiritual, and incorporeal. You are the temple of God in which God dwells, and you have within you that meat, that wine, that water which is spiritual and which is the substance of your external safety, security, abundance, and eternality. You have within you the substance of all form, the substance of everything necessary to the harmonious, joyous, abundant life.

Across the Desk

Joel tells us in many places that we must learn to "die daily." This term is often not understood, and in order really to do this "dying daily," we must seek for the meaning of it and understand why it is necessary for us to do this. Most of us know intellectually that what we are to "die" to is our humanhood, but we often fail to realize that this involves putting our spiritual life first and dropping our concern for the problems and activities of this world.

No longer are we permitted to seek Truth for healing, supply, ease, or comfort in this world. Our search now must be only for the purpose of rising higher into the realm of God-consciousness. This does not mean that we are to accept suffering in this world as necessary, but that the good we receive here will be the "added" things.

You will find that a study of "The Universality of God" in *The World Is New* will bring further enlightenment on this subject.

Tape Recorded Excerpts
Prepared by the Editor

Doubts are healthy, and certainly it is wise to question the measure of one's attained spiritual consciousness, rather than to rest back in smug satisfaction. Those who are seriously aspiring to attain spiritual illumination, however, usually find that they are not given much opportunity for any degree of smugness because all too often as they go deeper they are beset by more problems than ever before. It is then that they begin to wonder if they are on the wrong path or if there is any possibility of their ever attaining the hoped-for goal.

Such students will find it helpful to study the life of some of the great spiritual leaders. How much ease and freedom from problems did they really have? That is why most students will find the following excerpt comforting:

Is Human Harmony the Measure of Spiritual Attainment?

"You may have a few moments of emotion, ecstasy, or seeming to be on Cloud Nine, but there will always be an hour from now or tomorrow when that sense of separation breaks in because you can say to yourself, 'I cannot be one with God because I feel human. I even have a physical pain or a financial lack, and if I were one with God, this could not be.' . . .

"Do not judge from appearances. Do not judge from the fact that today you may be very ill or today you may be very poor or today you may be having sinful thoughts or today you may even be committing a sin. Do not judge from that as to whether or not you are one with God. All that can tell you is that at this moment you have a sense of separation from God. It cannot prove to you that you are not one with God. It might be true that you will go on being sick for awhile or being poor. It might even be true that you will go on having carnal thoughts or sinful appetites, and that you might even sometimes succumb to them. That may go on for a while, but do not let that fool you. . . .

"Actually, what happens is that we go along, sometimes for years, feeling that we are making absolutely no progress whatsoever. We . . . may not even have any outer sign of progress, and then all of a sudden, one day or one night in a split second, like Saul of Tarsus on the road to Damascus or like any of the mystics of whom we have read, it happens.

"So every mystic has discovered that he meditated, he studied, he practiced, he did whatever he was instructed to do in spite of not seeming to make much progress, and then . . . in one minute of one day or one second of one night, 'Whereas before I was blind, now I see,' and the 'old man' was dead, and the 'new man' was born."

Joel S. Goldsmith. "Consciously Attaining the Experience of Oneness," *The 1963 Kailua Private Class,* Reel III, Side I.

Chapter Ten

Let the Tares and the Wheat Grow Together

Another parable put he forth unto them, saying,
The kingdom of heaven is likened unto a man
which sowed good seed in his field:

But while men slept, his enemy came and sowed tares
among the wheat, and went his way.

But when the blade was sprung up, and brought
forth fruit, then appeared the tares also.

So the servants of the householder came and said
unto him, Sir, didst not thou sow good seed in thy
field? from whence then hath it tares?

He said unto them, An enemy hath done this.
The servants said unto him, Wilt thou then that we
go and gather them up?

But he said, Nay; lest while ye gather up the tares,
ye root up also the wheat with them.

> Let both grow together until the harvest: and in the
> time of harvest I will say to the reapers, Gather ye
> together first the tares, and bind them in bundles to
> burn them: but gather the wheat into my barn.
> Matthew 13:24-30

Most of the Bible is written in hidden or esoteric language and, to be understood, it must be spiritually interpreted. That is because, in the days of the Wisdom Schools, the Brotherhoods and all other organized activities that taught spiritual truth found it easier to teach by symbols than by outright everyday language. It has been proved throughout the centuries that whenever a profound subject is taught in plain language, ultimately it is lost, that is, the meaning is lost as well as the demonstration of the meaning. This has been particularly true of spiritual wisdom as found in scripture.

For many centuries the Bible has been read as if every statement were literally true. For example, Joshua is said to have made the sun stand still. "Sun, stand thou still. . . . So the sun stood still in the midst of heaven."[1] Behind that statement there is undoubtedly a spiritual truth, but the statement itself as it is written is not truth. Nobody has ever made the sun stand still; nobody ever will make the sun stand still.

There are passages of scripture that would undoubtedly make anyone wonder whether or not they are true. Did the Red Sea literally open for Moses to walk across? Did the Master look up and have a few loaves and fishes literally multiply themselves so that a whole multitude could eat, and twelve baskets full be left over? Is it literally true that the Master was taken from the crucifix, dead, entombed, and on the third day rose and walked the earth? Many of these questions must have come to your mind.

The religious writings of the world indicate that these questions have also come to the minds of scholars because there is a large literature on these subjects, some of which attempt to substantiate the miracles of the Bible and others to disprove them. As a matter of fact, efforts have been made trying to prove that Jesus Christ once lived and walked on this earth as if there were a very grave question about it. On the other hand, there is a considerable literature denying that there ever was such a man as Jesus.

Many questions such as these must come to your mind. If you are a student on the spiritual path, however, you will decide these things by an inner conviction. Because the kingdom of God is within you, the answer to every question is within you; the solution to every problem on earth is within you; and you can bring forth answers in the degree that you are willing to devote and dedicate yourself to that task.

Why Are So Few Prayers Answered?

One of the questions that must come to any thinking person is that if the sick can be healed through prayer, why is there so little healing through prayer in this world?

In the entire world, with its approximately four billion people, there is only a handful of metaphysical and spiritual healers, and even assuming that all of them do some healing work, that is a very small number compared with what is needed. There are millions of churches on earth, and most of these believe in the power of prayer, yet very few of them ever accomplish anything in the way of healing through prayer. Why is this? You will come to your own answer, but mine is that if a person prays and his prayers are not answered, he is praying amiss. My conviction is that the manner of praying, as most of us know it, is wrong.

How many millions of parents are praying for their children and how many thousands of ministers, priests, and rabbis are continually praying for the health of their congregations, and how little result is achieved in the way of healing! So the subject of healing through prayer resolves itself into this: either the idea that healing through prayer is possible must be given up or it must be clear that there is a way of praying that no one yet knows enough about.

From experience, I know that spiritual healing is not only a present possibility, but I also know that it is more to be relied upon than any other form of healing yet conceived by man. Then how are you to pray to bring this healing into your experience? And when I speak of healing, I mean how can the problems of human existence be dissolved. Whether they are problems of physical or mental disease, financial lack, discords of human relationships at any level—marital, filial, community, capital and labor, or international—whatever problems of human existence arise, they can be met by prayer.

The Master's life proved that he came to heal the sick, to raise the dead, to open the eyes of the blind, to open the ears of the deaf, to preach the gospel, and even to overcome the effects of storms and accidents. He embraced all the problems of human experience in his healing ministry. And so, too, when we speak of healing, we are really speaking of human problems in any form and of any degree.

Turning from This World to My Kingdom

As an experiment, take the passage, "My kingdom is not of this world."[2] These are the words of the Master. "My kingdom" must mean the kingdom of the son of God, the spiritual kingdom that is within you which is *not of this world*. At first it might seem that Jesus is saying that attaining this kingdom of God would have no effect upon your diseases, your lack, or your sins. But you have only to examine the Master's ministry to know that that would be a false assumption, as his ministry proved.

Whatever the name or nature of the problem that is

disturbing you most, whether it is one of your health or the health of a member of your family, whether it is a problem of supply or a problem of human relationships, for the next week or two, agree within yourself that every time this problem comes to your thought you will respond to it with "My kingdom is not of this world," and then refuse to treat that problem or that condition, refuse to take it to God, or try to bring God to it.

Do this every time the problem intrudes itself into your thought, and you may be assured that during the next week or two it is going to push at you much more than it ever has in the past. The very moment you try to ignore a thing, it hits you right over the head and tries to make you aware of it. So do not be surprised that your problem, whatever it is, lifts up its head when you are trying to ignore it, especially if you follow this procedure.

You are not going to take this problem to God, and you are not going to bring God to this problem. Your attitude is that *My* kingdom, the spiritual kingdom, the Christ kingdom, is not of this world, and therefore you are not going to take the problems of this world into heaven, nor are you going to try to bring the kingdom of heaven down to this problem.

You are going to rest confidently and securely in *My* kingdom and let the tares and the wheat grow side by side. That will be the second passage you will use to address to your problem: Let the tares and the wheat grow side by side. Be sure that you make no attempt to heal yourself. Make no attempt to overcome the erroneous condition. Make no attempt at all to meet it, but on the contrary, refuse to take it into consideration, because *My* kingdom has nothing to do with that problem, and that problem can never find entrance into the kingdom of God. So let the tares and the wheat grow side by side and see what happens.

This is not an easy assignment, and there will be times when you will wish you had never heard of this but had let sleeping dogs lie. If you are faithful, however, you will witness something you never dreamed of before, and that is that God is really "of purer eyes than to behold evil, and canst not look on iniquity."[3] There is no use in praying God to do something to your problems, because God does not know anything about your problems. What kind of a God would it be to have loose in the world if God solved the problems of any one individual and ignored all the other people who at the same time had problems! How can you believe that God can be influenced to heal your ills, while leaving all the others sick? It makes for some kind of a horrible God.

Resist Not Evil by Turning from Your Problem

Healing does not rest with God. It rests with you and your understanding of God and the nature of prayer. The Master said, "Resist not evil,"[4] and yet every attempt that you make to bring harmony into your life by trying to overcome, destroy, or do away with some evil is a resistance to the evil. You are plainly told, "Resist not evil." When you resist evil, you make the battle and the struggle more real. One way you have of seeing to what degree you can prove this is to leave your problem alone for the next few days and work in accord with this principle.

A friend of mine was a very well known and successful Christian Science practitioner. Every week he left his office Friday noon to go to one of his two ranches and came back Monday morning. He had no telephone at either one of his ranches. One day I said to him, "I don't quite understand how you can do this with a large practice such as you have. How can you not have some arrangement for your patients to be in touch with you over the weekend?"

He looked at me and said, "A funny thing, I've noticed, is that none of my patients dies while I'm away over the weekend. They wait for me to come home on Monday. There is no virtue in worrying about them. I leave them in the care of God—not in the care of man."

When you do not resist evil and let the tares and the wheat grow together, even if at first it seems frightening to do this and that apparently you are doing nothing, remember that you are trusting yourself to God. You are really trusting God to take hold of the situation while you are absent at your particular "ranch." Always remember that you can never be outside God's love, so you really need not fear to let the tares and the wheat grow together.

At every temptation to treat, to pray, or to meditate for a problem, resist the temptation in the realization of the non-power and nothingness of the problem. Turn from it, and figuratively go out to your "ranch." Your "ranch" can be a movie if you like, the television, a book, or anything that will prevent you from sitting down to pray about the particular problem. Your prayer is never to be about a problem. Prayer is always a tabernacling with what *is*. And remember always, "My kingdom is not of this world." Therefore, do not try to mix the kingdom of God with the temporal universe.

When you succeed in proving this principle, even in a small measure, you will know that the temporal kingdom is not something to be overcome or destroyed by God. It is to be realized as a mirage by man. God already knows God's kingdom. God already knows reality; God already knows immortality, eternality, and infinity. The only thing God knows nothing of is temporality, finiteness, mortality.

It lies with you to know the truth that will make you free. Do not believe that this leaves God out of your picture. On the contrary, this is the only way in which you honor God, because you are realizing that the kingdom of God is intact, that nothing can enter the kingdom of God that "defileth . . . or maketh a lie,"[5] and that anything unlike God was not made. Whatever is not of God is in the realm of a mythical kingdom, that Adamdream, temporality, mortality.

Neither the Master nor his great follower Paul taught that God should be brought into mortality. Instead they taught that mortality must be put off, "That mortality might be swallowed up of life."[6] We were told that we must "die daily."[7] No one was told by the Master to go to God and ask Him to heal his diseases. He was honoring God in the sense of knowing that His kingdom is intact. "This maiden is not dead, but sleepeth,"[8] or "Lazarus, come forth."[9] It is an assurance that harmony prevails.

Honor God by Recognizing His Kingdom Here and Now

Instead of trying to lift your problem up to God and get it into the mind of God so that He can do something about it, or instead of trying to bring the kingdom of God down into your mythical problem, recognize instantly:

> God's kingdom is not of this ephemeral world.
> God's kingdom is not in this belief in two powers.
> I know the truth, and the truth I know makes me
> free, the truth that all that God made is good.
> God made all that was made; therefore,
> this that I fight, battle, try to overcome or destroy,
> not being of God, was not made.

Your problems exist only in the same way that the mirage exists on the desert, as a misperception of what actually is.

"I will behold thy face in righteousness; I shall be satisfied, when I awake, with thy likeness."[10] You are not told that when you awaken you will heal anybody, but that you will see Him as He is, and that is perfect, perfect *now*.

The way to prove this and to pray in such a way as to honor God is to know that His kingdom is come on earth, as it is in heaven. His kingdom is established on earth, not will be in the future. God would not be God if He had a kingdom and kept it away from this earth now, and then was going to restore it later. God could not be God if God knew any harmony in the future tense. The only way God can be God is for His kingdom to be established where He is and when He is: now.

Instantaneous Healing, the Fruitage of Nowness

If you hearken well, you will also learn that in the kingdom of God there is neither time nor space. That is what makes instantaneous healing possible; that is what makes instantaneous reformation possible; that is what makes instantaneous forgiveness possible. There is no such thing as waiting in hell until your sins have been washed out; there is no such thing as waiting until you become pure; there is no such thing as waiting somewhere for something to happen, for that would take away from the instantaneity of God. That would take away from the omnipresence, omnipotence, and omniscience of God. Anything that has to do with a future tense would degrade our sense of God, for God cannot be God except *now,* and this *now* must be infinite, this *now* must be the omnipresence of God, nothing less and nothing else.

You honor God only in your realization of a timeless and ageless God. For this, you find authority in Scripture in such passages as "Thou art the same"[11] yesterday, today and forever. "I will never leave thee, nor forsake thee.[12] . . . I am with you alway, even unto the end of the world."[13] None of that indicates that there is any future tense in our relationship with God. Our relationship with God is now. "Now are we the sons of God,"[14] and if you cannot accept that, there is no way to accept the Christian teaching. "Know ye not that your body is the temple of the Holy Ghost?"[15] All this is now—not in the future. The

Master forgave the woman taken in adultery and the thief on the cross in a moment of nowness.

A New Way To Pray Without Ceasing

Do not go to God for anything, for that would be an indication that you wanted it in the future. Even if you expected it now, the fact that you are declaring that it was not there a moment ago is taking away from the instantaneity and the omnipresence of God. Instead of going to God, remember that God's kingdom is intact: now are you the son of God, and God's kingdom is not of this world. Then refuse to take this world to God. Refuse to take the pains of the flesh; refuse to take the lacks of the pocketbook; refuse to take the inharmonies of human relationships to God.

In doing this, you do not have to wait to sit down and close the eyes; you do not have to wait for a time of prayer. You can "pray without ceasing."[16] If you happen to be busy with cooking or housekeeping or if you are a businessman out about your business, you do not have to stop for one second, not even to close your eyes or to say a prayer. You can do whatever you are called upon to do and still think, "God's kingdom is not of this world, and I am not taking this world into God's kingdom. Therefore, let the tares and the wheat grow together."

This can be done twenty times a day, thirty or forty times. No time element enters into this, and no waiting. You will not wait until next Sunday to thank God. You will thank God where you are—in the tub, in the shower, in the bus, or at business, wherever you may be—and bring instantaneity into your experience, so that your life becomes a dedication to gratitude, for gratitude is that form of love which best expresses the qualities of love. And what do you have to be grateful for, if not the truth that God is, that God is now, that God is where you are, and that all of this exists in this glorious minute when now are we the sons of God!

As you let gratitude flow out from you for this joyous experience of realization, you then find how it is that love is a healer, that love is a way of life, that love is the Source of all life, and that this love best manifests itself through your gratitude. Your gratitude must not be because someone gave you something or because of some external condition: your gratitude must be that there is an infinite, invisible, spiritual kingdom which is intact. Once you separate this world from *My* kingdom, then this world starves and destroys itself. It becomes a nothingness because of its own nature.

Nowness Unfolds in Terms of Your Awareness

There must come a time in your experience when you do away with the future tense, when you do away with thinking about the good that is to come, the good that is desired, or the harmony that is hoped for. All this putting of things into the future is a human thing and not divine, and it does not have the sanction of Spirit. There is no way to reach spiritual harmony by *expecting* good. There is no way of reaping spiritual harmony by *expecting* harmony. There is no way of reaping or experiencing harmony in any other way than in understanding that whatever the appearance may be, harmony is. "Behold, now is the accepted time; behold, now is the day of salvation."[17] Now is when you are the child of God; now is when you are part of the spiritual kingdom; now is when the kingdom of God is established on earth.

Whether you are awake to it or whether you have overcome only seventy percent of the discords and are still working with the other thirty percent is not the point. This really means nothing. The only thing that counts is that you have a principle and that you work with this principle until you demonstrate it in its fullness. You are not going to demonstrate a pair of wings and a harp between now and next week. But it will be a wonderful thing if you have seen enough of this principle, even in some minor or seemingly insignificant way, so that at least you know you have found a principle and then have the coming months and years in which to prove this principle—but always from the standpoint of now, always from the standpoint of the word *is*.

As

If you go back go the book *The Infinite Way*, [18] you will find that there are two little words that are the foundation of Infinite Way work: the word "as" and the word "is." Those were the two words which were given to me originally. God is manifest *as* His son. God the Father is God the son, and God then is manifest as individual you and me. God is not something separate and apart from you and me, God is not something to be attained. God is to be realized. God is to be understood. *Now* "I and my Father are one,"[19] not after a period of life and death, but right now. God has made no provision in His kingdom for a future tense.

Now are you the son of God, and it is now that you must realize, "I and my Father are one. . . . Son, thou art ever with me." You can emphasize that word "ever." In fact, you could emphasize every word. "Son, thou art ever with me."[20] He is calling you "Son": "Son, thou art ever with me." You can take that entire passage and work with it until it rings in your ears that you can never be separate and apart from God. "Son, thou art ever with me, and all that I have is thine. . . . I and my Father are one." You are inseparable from God and indivisible. "He that seeth me seeth him that sent me."[21]

Is

As you dwell on this word "as," it naturally takes you the next step to the word "is":

God is my being: God is the life of me;
God is the mind of me; God is the soul of me;
God is the spirit of me. "For I shall yet praise him,
who is the health of my countenance, and my God." [22]
God is my fortress and high tower.

The whole Bible is made up of *is*. It is all *is*—no future tense. How many of us and how often do we cheat ourselves of the harmony that is waiting to flow into our experience because we cannot accept it as an *is!*

I think everyone is ready to accept this, if it will only come a minute from now. But it won't. That one minute of expectation separates you from it, because in the kingdom of God, there is nothing to be adjusted a minute from now. You might just as well expect God to adjust the tide a minute from now or make two times two equal four a minute from now. All that is, is a state of *is,* a state of divine Being now.

Whatever is not true of the divine Being now is never going to be true in the future. H_2O is water now, always has been, and always will be. All these laws of automotive engineering, of airplanes, all these laws of television and radio have always existed. Even when they were unknown, they did not exist in the future. They have always existed, as they exist now. They were only awaiting recognition, and when they were recognized, they were right here operating.

So it is with the law of God in your life. The law of God, of life, which of course must be the law of health and immortality, is operating in your experience, and there is no use praying for it. Praying for it will separate you from it. At least it will separate you in belief, but only in belief, because you cannot separate yourself from That which is. But you can separate yourself from It in experience, and the way to do that is to pray to God to do something for you, and see how far you separate yourself from what you are praying for.

When you understand that now God is the light unto your being, the lamp unto your feet, the health of your countenance, your fortress, and the life of your being, you keep the problem in its rightful place, out of your mind, and let those tares and wheat grow together. Then one of these mornings you awaken, and someone reminds you that there are no tares around you. There is only wheat. You will not know when your problems leave you until someone calls your attention to it.

Think of God as now. Think of the love of God as now and as being with you now. It makes no difference if right now you appear to be in some hell. It makes no difference if you appear to be going through "the valley of the shadow of death."²³ Make yourself realize that the love of God can have no future tense, or it would not be God in action, for God is omnipresence, and where the presence of God is, there is liberty. And the presence of God is wherever the presence of God is realized.

Across the Desk

By this time, most of you will have received and begun to study the new book by Joel, *The Mystical* I. The publication of this book is of special significance to students of the Infinite Way since in it the revelation of "the unveiling" has been released to the general public. Joel taught the nature of the unveiling in a number of classes, and these classes have been available to serious students on the tape recordings, but now it is possible for anyone to secure this book and study its meaning.

In *The Mystical* I, the veil of personalization is stripped aside, and God is revealed as individual being, as being the heart and soul of every individual, and not only in one or in a few spiritual teachers throughout the ages, but in every individual. Those of us who love the Infinite Way must be in the vanguard of those who heed Joel's insistent admonitions in this respect when he wrote:

When I unveil the truth of the *I* of your being as God, the son of God, and Christ as the mediator, the individualization, the connecting link between *I,* the Father, and *I,* the son, I am revealing the truth that sets you free. Should some students in the future claim that Joel is their master, you will recognize what they are doing. They are putting the veil back on the truth: somebody either wants to get rich or powerful, or somebody is very stupid. It has to be either an evil purpose or it has to be stupidity.

Some have put the veil back on the truth through stupidity, through ignorance of the meaning of the word *I,* and through personalizing It. Others have put the veil on ignorantly by trying to worship somebody and thinking that was humility. But what is true humility? Humility is recognizing that a spiritual teacher is the Christ of God. That is humility because it leads to the next truth, "And so am I." But to say that only one man is the Christ of God is not humility; it is stupidity. . . . I have not been setting myself apart, . . . but have been revealing that every truth spoken about Jesus Christ or any of the saints or sages of the past or present is the truth to be realized about every person.[1]

*Tape Recorded Excerpts
Prepared by the Editor*

To resist the temptation to change the human scene calls for a sturdy kind of spiritual stamina which stems from the realization that the realm of *I,* in which we are to dwell, is "My kingdom." So what have we to do with "this world"? To try to improve this world is to exchange a bad concept for a good one, at best, and that is not the spiritual kingdom in which there is neither good nor evil, but only eternal perfection. Our work is not to exchange one picture for another, but to climb up into "My kingdom," the realm of harmony and eternality.

My Kingdom Is Not of This World

"You are not to battle evil or try to overcome it: you are to sit back in quietness and in confidence and realize: God alone is power. All of this that has been troubling me is the appearance with which I have been battling and which I cannot win over because it isn't really there. I am maintaining it in my own thought as a mental image by fighting it; whereas by relaxing 'in quietness and in confidence,' I can realize that this picture that is confronting me is a picture, not a person, although it may appear as a person. The appearance may testify to its being a person or the appearance may testify to its being a condition, but I have to realize that it is neither a person nor a condition but an appearance.

"This brings us to the place where you never look at a human being with the idea of changing his evil into good, his disease into health, his lack into abundance. You could do this in some of the mental sciences, but you cannot do this in a mystical teaching or spiritual teaching. . . . You do not look at a human and seek to make his evil good, his lack into abundance, his sin into purity. What you do is to look through the appearance and realize: Unseen to my human eye, this is the Christ, the son of God; and I do not seek to change it, improve it, reform it, or enrich it. I look right through the appearance and remember that even though I cannot see it, here is spiritual identity.

"While this is not too difficult when you are beholding an erroneous human appearance, the reason you do not have greater success is that you do not do it when you see a good human appearance—and you must. When you see a healthy person or a wealthy person or a successful person or a happy person, you cannot rejoice in that because tomorrow the whole picture may be turned upside down. It can be reversed in an hour, and then you will say, 'What was I rejoicing about?'"

Joel S. Goldsmith. " 'This World' and 'My Kingdom'," *The 1960 Second London Closed Class,* Reel I, Side I.

"To pray aright means insofar as possible to put the problem aside and start with a realization: "God's kingdom is not of "this world," so there is no use in my praying for anything in this world or of this world. Father, let me pray for something that is of Thy kingdom. It is the grace of Thy kingdom that I seek. . . .

"We have all witnessed people who thought they were healthy, and then all of a sudden on a checkup found they were very ill with things that had been going on for years of which they were not aware. There is no use praying for something of this world when even if we seem to have it, we find out later that we do not have it.

"Our function in this work is to learn what the kingdom of God consists of. 'Seek ye first the kingdom of God, and all these things will be added unto you': the health will come—this we all know from experience—the supply comes, the companionship comes, the home comes, the joys come. They all come, but not by taking thought, not by praying for them, but by dropping these things out of our thoughts and letting God take care of them in God's own way and centering our attention on: What is the kingdom of God? What was the Master teaching when he said, 'My kingdom is not of this world'? What did Isaiah mean when he said, 'Cease ye from man, whose breath is in his nostrils: for wherein is he to be accounted of '? The human being is that 'man, whose breath is in his nostrils.' Why, then, should we take thought about making him better, healthier, or richer? Why take thought for 'man, whose breath is in his nostrils' when we can take thought about the son of God? What is the son of God? . . .

"The most difficult step on the spiritual path is when you are about to bring yourself to the place of not praying for things, conditions, or circumstances, because the moment you come to that decision, all the material things and thoughts in the world rise up to tempt you. All the lacks and limitations rise up to tempt you. Everything seems to conspire to drop you back. If you don't think so, open your Bible at the Master's three temptations and see how even after he was a Master, even after he was recognized as the Christ, he had to go through three temptations that rose up in an attempt to pull him down from his spiritual height. But he had the spiritual stamina, he had the spiritual vision that enabled him to be very calm and say, 'Get thee behind me, Satan.' He recognized them as temptations, and he knew that if he turned stones into bread, or attempted to, he was forfeiting divine aid. He knew that if he accepted the temptation to glorify his human selfhood or to prove that he had miraculous powers that he would be forfeiting divine aid. . . .

"You will find, when you have taken your stand to put away the temptation to pray for things, conditions, or circumstances, and to make your life of prayer one of spiritual seeking, one of seeking for spiritual enlightenment, one of the seeking of spiritual grace, one of praying for the understanding of the nature of spiritual riches, spiritual health, spiritual harmony, and spiritual completeness, how difficult it is."

Joel S. Goldsmith. "Prayer, Spiritually Understood,"
The 1960 Manchester Closed Class, Reel III, Side 1.

Chapter Eleven

Sowing and Reaping

> Be not deceived; God is not mocked:
> for whatsoever a man soweth,
> that shall he also reap.
>
> Galatians 6:7

Deep meditation on a biblical passage such as this reveals that we ourselves set in motion the blessings and the punishment that we receive. There is no God doing this to us, and there is no devil doing it to us either, but we ourselves set in motion both the blessings and the punishment.

Punishment comes from believing that profit or satisfaction is to be found somewhere outside our own being. As long as we entertain that belief, we can be punished for it, whether or not it is ever externalized. Did not the Master say that it is just as sinful to look on a woman with lust as it is to commit adultery? That is because the act itself, once it is done is over and finished; but the inner desire, the false desire for a satisfaction or an activity apart from God or for supply apart from God is a sin within our own being, and as long as that is there, the punishment is there. The punishment is for the belief we have accepted of a selfhood apart from God, the belief of an incomplete selfhood. We would be punished for that if we never sinned in the outer realm. But how do we overcome that? By realizing our true identity and by realizing that we live by Grace and not by outer satisfactions.

As *ye* sow, not as God sows and not as the devil sows, but as *ye* sow, so shall *ye* reap. When we are sowing to the Spirit, we are, of course, sowing to truth and to love. In meditation and prayer, we set in motion the law of love through forgiveness, through praying for the enemy, through loving our neighbor as ourselves, through doing unto others as we would have them do unto us. Thereby we are sowing seeds of love and seeds of truth. In that sowing, the soil is being prepared for spiritual reaping, because with no devil to interfere and no God to give or withhold, we are going to reap what we have sown.

Setting in Motion the Law of Love

In Christian mysticism, this teaching is called the law of as-ye-sow-so-shall-ye-reap; in Oriental mysticism, it is called the law of karma. They both mean the same thing; the law of cause and effect. The cause that we set in motion through forgiveness is love, and therefore the effect must be love. If the bread that we have cast on the water is love, truth, and blessing, the bread that will return unto us will be of that same nature.

There is no other way to pray than to sow the seeds of truth, life, and love, to set in motion the law of love, and then watch how our prayer is answered spiritually. In the past, we have sown to the flesh, sown seeds of resentment, anger, intolerance, bias, bigotry, dishonesty, falsehood: all seeds of mental malpractice. In some measure, this is exactly what life has paid back to us in the form of sin, false appetite, lack, limitation, and the penalty of being misunderstood.

Fortunately, the entire Christian dispensation was given to us in order that we might set aside the law. The law came by

Moses, but grace and truth came by the Christian dispensation of Christ Jesus. This means that at any moment that we repent, as we do in meditations of forgiveness, in retracting every bit of erroneous belief we have held about others, and in withdrawing from circulation all hate, envy, jealousy, malice, bias, bigotry, in that moment of repentance, we have removed ourselves from under the law and have brought ourselves under Grace.

Coming Under Grace

To be brought under Grace is an act of consciousness, and one which we individually and specifically must perform. It is not done for us. No, the act of moving from being under the law to being under Grace is an act of repentance. It is the acknowledgment within ourselves of our mistakes and our wrongdoing and a turning to a sowing to the Spirit: to truth, to life, to love.

In a moment of selfless meditation, we uproot the law of the fruits of our former acts of corruption. We perform our act of repentance; we turn from the human way of thinking, judging, and valuing; we turn to the spiritual way and sow seeds of truth, life, and love. Then, we come under Grace. At every moment of our existence we are either placing ourselves under the law or maintaining ourselves under Grace.

Can you imagine the look in the eyes of the woman taken in adultery as she stood before her accusers, that look directed at the Master that demanded, asked for, and pleaded for understanding and forgiveness, even without saying a word? And the Master answered, "Neither do I condemn thee: go, and sin no more."[1] Just her look convinced the Master of her repentance, and the past was wiped out. Instantly! No period of sorrow, no period of grief, no period of going through Hades, but wiped out in a moment, because there was no condemnation, nor is there ever any condemnation from the Christ. There is forgiveness, and with it a warning: "Go, and sin no more."

In other words, in the moment of repentance, in the moment of sowing the seeds of life, truth, and love, we are absolved from the law of punishment, we are forgiven our sins, and we are under Grace. But we are reminded, "'Go, and sin no more.' Do not go back tonight or tomorrow to criticizing, judging, and condemning. Do not go back tomorrow to judging after the flesh."

To be under Grace does not mean that we are not aware of the sins that are being committed in the world. It means that, instead of sitting in judgment on them and wanting to be the means of punishing them, we understand that man sins only because of his ignorance. He knows not what he does. Seventy times seven, therefore, we can say within ourselves to every form of evil that we behold, "Neither do I condemn thee. As far as I am concerned, thy sins be forgiven thee." In that way, we are maintaining ourselves under Grace.

I have seen a thousand times, in the practice, that sins, even sins of commission, were not punished once the realization had come to an individual of the truth of life by Grace. The whole difference lies in the realization of living by Grace as against the belief of living by virtue of some outer circumstance, condition, person, or activity.

The man whose being is in Christ is the man who lives in spiritual awareness rather than living out from person, place, thing, circumstances, or conditions in the outer world.

> Thank you, Father; I already am. There is nothing
> to be desired; there are no changes and no
> adjustments necessary; there is nothing to be
> patched up or fixed up. Every moment Thou art my
> Grace, so even without my planning or taking
> thought, It flows and produces the manna as it is
> necessary: the manna of companionship, satisfaction,

joy, money, transportation, or whatever is
needed according to human belief.

Each one nullifies the power of karma or the law of as-ye-sow-so-shall-ye-reap the moment he stops sowing and the moment he begins to have his being in Christ. To have one's being in Christ is to understand the great words:

Thank you, Father; I am—not will be, not shall be,
and not deserve to be. All that You have is mine.
I live and move and have my being in Your divine
consciousness, and as of this moment, Life fulfills
Itself through me. Life lives Itself through me as me;
Life flows; and I am a beholder of Its activity.

In that meditation, you have wiped out all punishment for past actions because you have died to the man who committed the sin and you have been reborn into the new being. Many of you may remember that there was a time when perhaps you smoked and drank and had a healing and then tomorrow you did not smoke and drink and you were not the same person. If you looked in the mirror, you were, but to yourself you were not because now you wonder how those things could ever have held you in bondage.

Putting Faith in the Creation
Rather Than the Creator

Sowing to the flesh means that we put our faith and trust in that which is manifest as form or creation, and this means that we are loving the creation more than the Creator. We might take the subject of money as an example. We all know that God never made money. Money is an object of exchange, a creation of man. What happens to our soul if we either love, hate, or fear money? What does it do to our soul if, instead of loving the Lord our God supremely, instead of trusting in Spirit, divine Cause, we say, "Oh, no, money is my supply; money is my need. Money is what I fear, either to have too much or too little. Money is that which I love and must have." Money is not only a creation, but it is a man-made creation, and to give it power of any kind is sowing to the flesh.

Sowing to the Spirit

We shall have life and peace if we understand Spirit to be the substance of our good. If we understand Spirit as the life of our body, as the capital, the working tools, and the drawing power of our business, if we understand Spirit as the law of fulfillment in every department of our business, every activity of our body, every aspect of our home life, then we are no longer sowing to the flesh, that is, looking to manifested form: we are sowing to the Spirit and we reap life everlasting.

The man who is living the human sense of life cannot please God. He cannot find his attunement or at-onement with God because he is seeking his good in the outer realm, in the realm of effect, instead of in the realm of cause. In other words, he may be storing up manna for tomorrow, failing to recognize that manna has its source in one's individual consciousness and, therefore, he carries it with him and permits it to fall anew every day. To lay up manna for tomorrow is to be under the law of limitation, but a person is under Grace when he realizes that if that manna flows today as the activity of God, it must be an eternal flow, and therefore he is not under the law of limitation, the law of hoarding, or the law of looking to yesterday's manna.

To be under Grace means to live under the gift of God or the love of God, and that means to be supplied every moment. Inasmuch as our individual consciousness is this law of Grace, this law of supply, we can see then that a belief such as karma or as-ye-sow-so-shall-ye-reap can be nullified.

It is sowing to the Spirit when we value money only for its use, respect it for its purpose, but at the same time we look always to the Spirit for our supply. To love, to hate, or to fear money is to sow to the flesh, and out of such idolatry we reap corruption.

> I look to the Source, the Creator,
> not the created thing. I put my faith, my hope,
> and my trust in the invisible Substance,
> not in the form that it assumes out here.

Faith in Persons or in the Creator?

We are told to "cease ye from man, whose breath is in his nostrils: for wherein is he to be accounted of."[2] Yet what faith we often place in man! Too often we place our trust in persons instead of in God, the Author, the Creator of all. How often we fear persons and what they might do to us! In doing so, we are sowing to the flesh. If we want to fear, let us fear to do wrong, and let us not fear man. If we are to love, let us love the Lord our God with all our heart, with all our soul, and with all our might. This does not eliminate human affection or human love. It eliminates the love, the trust, and the faith in mankind instead of in the Creator.

Unconsciously, we think of the person who at the moment is the channel of our supply, or we look at the particular position we have in life, the firm we work for or someone's favor, and we cater to "man, whose breath is in his nostrils," as if man could give or withhold our supply. Thereby, we are sowing to the flesh.

To sow to the Spirit means to honor and respect those with whom we live and work, those who are sharing with us, those who are the avenues or channels of our supply, always remembering, "Ah, yes, I am thankful to you as an instrument, as a channel for my immediate supply, but I recognize God, Spirit, as the Source. Therefore, I know that if one door closes, another door opens. If one avenue of supply is closed, another opens, because I am not putting my faith or trust in the immediate avenue, but in the Source, the spiritual creative principle."

The moment we look behind the particular avenue or channel and realize, "Yes, you are at this moment the avenue of my supply, and while I am grateful to you for fulfilling that function, my hope, dependence, and reliance are not on you, but on God, the invisible Source of all good," we are sowing to the Spirit, and through that sowing, we reap infinite supply.

Never must we put our faith and trust in that which has form, figure, or outline, in other words, in that which is created. Our faith, hope, and trust are always in the Infinite Invisible, the kingdom which is within our own being. In such a state of consciousness, we are no longer under the law of supply and demand; we are no longer under the law of economics; we are no longer under the law of the amount of our supply of gold, silver, or currency. We have brought ourselves out from under the law and placed ourselves under Grace, but this must be done as a specific act of our own consciousness.

In our meditation, we respect and honor and thank all those who are the instruments of supply to us. We shall ever be grateful to anyone who at any time has ever been a part of our supply, but always we recognize that they were and are but instruments, that behind them is the Source, and we hear It saying to us, " 'Son, . . . thou art ever with me.'³ Do not fear fleshly man. 'Thou art ever with me, and all that I have is thine.' "³

Sowing to the Spirit Results in Reaping the Life More Abundant

To bring ourselves under Grace, let us listen to what the Master has to say to us. If we know how to listen and are able to hear it, we will bring ourselves out from under the law of boom seasons and depressions, out from under the law of the man of earth, and we will place ourselves under Grace.

Now hear this; "I am come that they might have life, and that they might have it more abundantly."[4] Hear it again: "I am come." This is not a husband or wife talking; this is not our employer; this is not our social security; this is not our bonds, stocks, or real estate talking. This is *I*. "I am come that they might have life, and that they might have it more abundantly"—not husband, wife, parents, inheritances, or securities, but *I* am come. In this instant, let us transfer all our hope and faith and reliance from the outer world to the *I*.

> *I* am thy bread, meat, wine, and water. *I* am the
> resurrection, the law of renewal. *I* in the midst of you
> am mighty, and *I* will not leave you or forsake you.

> *I* have been with you since "before Abraham was." [5]
> *I* have been with you since the beginning of the
> world, but you have ignored *Me* and instead
> you have depended on this world.

In a moment of repentance, in a moment of sowing to the Spirit, let us turn within and listen and understand:

> I am come that you might have life. I am thy bread,
> thy wine, and thy water. I am thy food, thy clothing,
> and thy housing.

> In times of danger, *I* am the rock on which you are to
> stand. *I* am the fortress in which you are to abide.
> You are to live, and move, and have your being in
> *Me*. Let *Me* be your dwelling place. Do not concern
> yourself with needing an apartment or a house.

> *I* promise you these things will be added unto you if
> you will abide in *Me*, if you will make Me your
> dwelling place, if you will abide in *I*.

Morning, noon, and night, repeat the word *I*, with a smile
on your lips:

> *I* am "closer. . . than breathing, and nearer than
> hands and feet," [6] and *I* in the midst of me am the
> life and the resurrection. *I* in the midst of me, *I* am
> life eternal. *I* do not have to look to a book or to
> man for my life. *I* dwell in the *I* within me; *I* draw
> my life from the *I* that is within me, my sustenance,
> my protection. *I* will never leave me, nor forsake me.
> *I* will be with me unto the end of the world.

Let us withdraw our gaze from this world, draw back from
trusting those dollars in our pocket or in the bank, withdraw
our trust, hope, and faith in our savings, in our investments, in
our social security and our government, draw back every bit of
faith and place it where it belongs: in *I*, the *I* that will never
leave us, the *I* that is our bread, meat, wine, and water, the *I* that
will be with us unto the end of the world, the *I* that is our life
and the resurrection of our life.

Efficacious Prayer

In order to sow to the Spirit, we know that we must place
our hope, faith, reliance, and remembrance in the *I* that is within us. Then we are praying spiritually, praying the prayer of a
righteous man, the prayer that is efficacious, the prayer that
availeth much. We are knowing the truth that makes us free,
free of human domination, free of human dependence, free of
human limitation. Knowing the truth establishes our oneness

with the Father, oneness with our Source. Now we are under Grace. By an act of our consciousness, we have taken ourselves out from under the law of matter, the law of man, the law of time and space, and have placed ourselves under divine Grace, under Christ.

"I can do all things through Christ which strengtheneth me.[7]. . . I live; yet not I, but Christ liveth in me."[8] It is this Christ, this *I,* which is our life, this *I* that has come to give us the life more abundant. Now we live through It—not through circumstances or conditions. Now we are not the man of earth; now we are that man who has his being in Christ, who lives by and through Spirit, who having sown to the Spirit now lives and reaps spiritually, infinitely, abundantly, graciously. But this is only while we are abiding in love, because we cannot fool the principle of life.

We cannot in one breath sow to the flesh, indulge in a mental malpractice of this world, and in the next breath expect to be under the grace of spiritual Influence. In order to be under Grace, we must live spiritually, and that does not mean any denial of the ordinary human modes of living. It means only a denial of the satisfaction of malpracticing our neighbor instead of loving our neighbor.

No longer are we under "an eye for an eye, and a tooth for a tooth"[9]—the Hebraic law. No longer are we under fear. When we are under Grace and our entire reliance is on the *I* that is within us, how can we fear man? How can we fear times and conditions? It is impossible! If we are under Grace, the law of man has no power over us. This is demonstrated in the life of all those who have brought themselves under Grace and have found then that the man-made laws of life no longer function.

We live through the Christ, this Spirit that dwells in us, whose name is *I,* but remember, no longer are we to expect It to go out and destroy our enemies, no longer are we to expect It to destroy our competitors, either domestic or foreign. No longer do we expect It to prosper us at the expense of someone else. Now, as we look to this *I* that has come to give us life, the life more abundant, let us remember that we are at the same moment praying this prayer for our neighbor, for our competitor, for our enemy, praying that the grace of God be equally upon them. That they themselves may not know it or benefit by it is not our concern. No, our concern is to know the truth; our function is to pray for our enemy, for our competitor, for our neighbor, as we would have them pray for us, if only they would.

The Christ Destroys the Mortal and Material Tendencies in Us

The function of the Christ that is within us is not to go out and destroy anything or anybody in this world, but It is to overcome the mortal and material tendencies in us. In our prayer, therefore, we are always praying that the Christ dissolve whatever is left of mortality and materiality in our consciousness. We are not praying for the Christ to do anything to change anybody, only to resurrect us out of the tomb of mortality, and as a further step also to resurrect our friendly or unfriendly neighbor out of the tomb of his materiality. Our prayer is that the Christ raise us from the tomb of mortality, that Christ raise mankind from the tomb of mortality and materiality. This is our prayer, and this is the prayer that availeth much.

We have been so ignorant on the subject of prayer that now it becomes necessary for us to retrace two thousand years of error, to go back to the source of our instruction in prayer and learn how to pray again. We begin now with the attitude that these two thousand years of erroneous praying can be wiped out, as indeed they can be, in a moment. They can be wiped out in this moment, if only we understand that *I* will never leave us nor forsake us, and that *I* is the source of our good. *I* is the source of our supply; *I* is the source of our health. This enables us to close the eyes and see the fountain of good that is within us. This keeps us from sowing to the flesh and enables us to stop looking to man for justice, for mercy, and seek it where it is to be found.

"Neither do I condemn thee." Can we for a moment hear within ourselves this Voice speaking to us and saying, from within our own being: "Neither do I condemn thee?"

Your sins are forgiven you; you are
under Grace; go, and sin no more.

The place whereon you stand is holy ground
because *I* am here with you. If you mount up to
heaven, *I* will be with you. If for any reason you
temporarily make your bed in hell, do not be
discouraged or give up. *I* am also there with you to
resurrect you from any hell of sin or disease.

Only turn to *Me*; turn to *Me*. *I* will not forsake you. *I*
am closer to you when you are in sin, disease, poverty, and death than when you are well and prosperous,
because it is only in your lack and limitation that you
turn deeply and wholeheartedly to the *Me* that is
within you, awaiting your recognition.

Bless this problem that has turned your thought to
Me. Pray that this problem will be not solved until
you have once again been reunited with *Me* in Spirit
and recognized *Me* as your life and your supply,
I am your bread; you will never hunger.

I am the health of your countenance—not that bottle
of medicine out there and certainly not that knife in
a surgeon's hands. *I* am the health of your

countenance, and *I* will never leave you or
forsake you. Turn to *Me*.

"Cease ye from man, whose breath is in his nostrils."
Do not worship the creation more than the
Creator. Do not look to that which man has
created for your blessing, but look to *Me*.

Giving God the First Fruits

Whatever form of good comes to us, let us be thankful and
give God the first fruits. It is only as we love our neighbor as
ourselves that we are giving the first fruits to God. If we are
blessed, let us be sure to share it with those who have not yet
awakened to their blessings. To give always the first fruits to
God is our sign of love; it is our sign of loving our neighbor as
ourselves and loving God supremely, because the only way we
can ever love God is by loving our neighbor.

"Inasmuch as ye have done it unto one of the least of
these my brethren, ye have done it unto me." [10]
When you feed a hungry one, you are bringing
bread to *Me*. When you comfort the comfortless,
you are comforting *Me*.

I am come that you might have life.
All of the life harmonious that you want,
you must find through *Me*. You must find it by
realizing that *I* in the midst of you is the Christ.

Loving Restores Us to the Divine Consciousness

We have prayed spiritually when we have prayed the prayer
of love, truth, and forgiveness; and in doing this, we have sown

to the Spirit. We have made sure that now we will reap the Spirit. As we sow tonight, tomorrow morning, tomorrow noon, tomorrow night, so will we reap. As we sow these seeds of love, truth, and life, as we continue this sowing morning, noon, and night, day after day, night after night, unto the end of our days, so will we reap life everlasting.

> "I live; yet not I, but Christ liveth my life."
> The Christ goes before me to make "the crooked
> places straight," [11] to make mansions for me, and It
> walks beside me as my protection. This infinite
> invisible *I*, this divine Source that is within me, this
> is the Christ that forgives me; this is the Christ that
> redeems me; this is the Christ that feeds me; this is
> the Christ that raises me from the tomb of mortality
> into the realm of immortality, of life eternal.

In our oneness with the Father, I am in you, and you are in me, and we are one in God. We are united in the divine consciousness of the spirit of God; we are united in His love, if so be we keep loving. If we would bring upon ourselves this divine consciousness in which we find ourselves when we are loving, we have only to return to this silence and reunite ourselves consciously with this same Spirit that is flowing through us now. The same Spirit of love which envelops those of us who are immersed in the Spirit now can be ours for the rest of our days, on this plane and on the next one to come, as we reunite ourselves in this same consciousness of love, praying this same prayer that we have prayed.

We are of the household of God. As we look out upon our world—the world of our business, our home, the streets—we remember that even though many of the persons we encounter may not know it, they also are of the household of God, and we are knowing that truth for them. We are removing from them the power of a universal malpractice that says that they are mortals. We are removing from them this universal mesmerism of fear, just by including them in our spiritual household, in our spiritual consciousness.

We address any picture in the human scene, as Jesus did once: "Be of good cheer; it is I; be not afraid."[12] Any and every situation we address with "Be not afraid, it is I." This is realizing the presence of God, and where that realization is, there is freedom.

Across the Desk

As we approach a period of nationwide Thanksgiving, it would be wise to contemplate the meaning of this term used so freely and indiscriminately. The commonly accepted sense of Thanksgiving means, quite simply, giving thanks or showing gratitude for our blessings, and in *Practicing the Presence* Joel writes, "Gratitude is the sharing or expressing of joy for the good already received."

What is that good? Are we thinking of that good or those blessings as merely material things or happy human experiences? Is it the changing human scene, good today and bad tomorrow, or is that good something much deeper and more basic than that, a spiritual gift? That good was received in the beginning because God's gift of Grace is planted in us from everlasting to everlasting.

Joel goes on to speak of gratitude as "a giving without a single sigh, without a single trace of desire for a return." Does not this show us that thanksgiving, which is gratitude expressed, must be a pouring out process, a giving forth to the world of that gift of peace, light, and joy which will raise the consciousness of all mankind? How much gratitude will you permit to be expressed through you? Have a real Thanksgiving!

Tape Recorded Excerpts
Prepared by the Editor

On the human level of life, karma acts as an irrevocable law which no human being can break. Its operation is inexorable. The spiritual path, however, is the journey from that level to the high altitude of spiritual consciousness where karma no longer operates because the only doer is *I*.

The following excerpts from the tape recordings will help to clarify your understanding of this subject which has held so many in bondage and will show you how karma is surmounted.

Karma

"Karmic law in the Christian world is called the law of as-ye-sow-shall-ye-reap. Sowing, when it is outside of the rhythm of the universe, which means that it is outside of the obedience to the two commandments, this alone creates karmic law, and there is no setting aside of that karmic law, even if you were to wait ten generations. Karmic law is set aside in any given moment when you return to the rhythm of the universe by obeying the two commandments. . . .

"This you do in silence. You do not do it by speech. In the silence acknowledge: *I* am God, the *I* of my being, 'closer. . . to me than breathing,' and It, the *I* of me, is Omniscience, the all-knowing. Therefore whatever wisdom I seek, I seek by sitting in the silence and letting It impart Itself to me. Whatever strength I need, I receive by sitting in the silence and letting This that is 'closer. . . to me than breathing' bestow Itself upon me."

Joel S. Goldsmith. "An Act of Commitment; The Womb of Creation," *The 1964 London Studio Class,* Reel II, Side 1.

"If we violate a moral or a spiritual law, even if no one knows about it. . . we have put in motion a karmic law, or the law of as-ye-sow-so-shall-ye-reap. Sooner or later, our error will find us out and demand payment. We have come to look upon this as punishment, almost as if it were punishment from God. . . . It is a punishment from our ignorance, entirely due to our ignorance, and the punishment ends in the very moment of our enlightenment.

"*I* in the midst of thee am mighty. . . . That mightiness could be brought into the external realm by our taking the attitude of a beholder and being completely still in the presence of the *I* that I am. It is this *I* against which our human thoughts hit when the human part of us indulges in the human hates, human loves, human fears, human doubts, human ignorance. When this hits up against that *I,* it rebounds as what we call punishment which isn't punishment at all: it is just the natural error that is born of error.

"Karmic law is set in motion whenever a human sentiment hits up against the spiritual reality of the *I* that I am. The moment Joel thinks a wrong thought or does a wrong deed, this has hit up against his inner spiritual integrity and bounces back at him. Because the results are not always visible at the same moment, we sometimes think that we can escape it, but inevitably it reaches us, and then we say afterwards, 'Why do I suffer from this? Why did this have to happen to me?' We have forgotten the law that we set in motion by violating our own spiritual integrity. Fortunately, we can correct this at any time by withdrawing the personal sense of self that loves, hates, or fears, and becoming beholders as we stand in the presence of the Spirit, the *I* that is within us. This absolves us from all our previous mistakes and the penalties thereof."

Joel S. Goldsmith. "An Act of Worship and the Fruitage," *The 1964 London Studio Class,* Reel II, Side 2.

Chapter Twelve

The Message of the Bible

The state of consciousness you are, the elevation of consciousness you attain, this determines what manner of life you lead. It determines whether you live the life of a grubworm, of a slave, or a free man, or the life of a spiritual entity. It all depends upon what your state of consciousness is.

In one state of consciousness, you could very well have been a slave and had everybody ordering you about. But as, through Grace, a higher realization came, you asserted your dominion and became a free man—still human, but free. As greater light came and your consciousness changed, you realized, "I am not merely a free man. I am a spiritual man. I have God-given strength, God-given dominion, and God-given freedom."

Eventually you will reach the place in consciousness where Jesus was when he said, "He that seeth me seeth him that sent me."[1] Jesus had not always been at that stage. At one time he was at the state of other Hebrew rabbis in the temple, but he grew until he came to the passage where he read from the book of Isaiah and said, "The spirit of the Lord is upon me, because he hath anointed me to preach the gospel to the poor; he hath sent me to heal the brokenhearted, to preach deliverance to the captives, and recovering of sight to the blind, to set at liberty them that are bruised. . . . This day is this scripture fulfilled in your ears."[2] With that, he realized, "Why, no, I'm not going to stand on a platform just reading out of a book." So he stepped down from that platform and went out into the world, not as a temple rabbi but as a world rabbi. Later, all that passed from him, and he was no longer a rabbi: he was a Master.

So it is that one day you are addressed as housewife or businessman, then one day as a practitioner, and later as teacher. If you keep ascending in consciousness, one day you will be addressed as Master. It all depends on your state of consciousness. If you have advanced to this point, you are already on the spiritual path. If you do not become satisfied when you find yourself healthy and with enough supply and believe that you have arrived, but instead keep going on, then one day you will not call yourself a housewife or businessman and neither will anybody else, but others will be thinking of you as their practitioner, and then someday they will think of you as their teacher. If you keep on going forward, there is no limit to where you can go because there is no limit to consciousness.

Of Ourselves, We Are Nothing

In the Bible, there are sixty-six books written by Hebrews who were undoubtedly in various states and stages of consciousness. Nevertheless, they all tell the same story, and that story is of That which is invisible, so that you and I do not think too highly of ourselves and remember with humility that, regardless of what we may be or what heights we may attain, it is only accomplished by the grace of God and through the presence and the power of God. You and I of ourselves as men and women are nothing, but by the Grace that flows through us, we will see what we are.

> The words of Jeremiah the son of Hilkiah,
> of the priests that were in Anathoth
> in the land of Benjamin:

> To whom the word of the Lord came in the days of
> Josiah the son of Amon king of Judah.
>
> Jeremiah 1:1,2

Did you notice this: "to whom the word of the Lord came"? There is the beginning of the secret of the message of the Bible. The word of the Lord must come in order to lift you out of the ranks of being nothing but an ordinary man or woman, the mass, the rabble, because that is all anyone is of himself until the word of the Lord comes. Then something happens.

As you read the following passage, will you try to reach back inside yourself as if a voice inside were saying this to you? In that way, you will catch the meaning of it. The word of the Lord now is speaking to you, and it is saying:

> Then the word of the Lord came unto me, saying,
> Before I formed thee in the belly I knew thee;
> and before thou camest forth out of the womb
> I sanctified thee, and I ordained thee a
> prophet unto the nations.
> Then said I, Ah, Lord God! behold,
> I cannot speak: for I am a child.
> But the Lord said unto me, Say not,
> I am a child: for thou shalt go to all that
> I shall send thee, and whatsoever I
> command thee thou shalt speak.
> Be not afraid of their faces:
> for I am with thee to deliver thee, saith the Lord.
> Then the Lord put forth his hand,
> and touched my mouth. And the Lord said unto me,

Behold, I have put my words in thy mouth.
See, I have this day set thee over the nations and over
the kingdoms, to root out, and to pull down, and to
destroy, and to throw down, to build, and to plant.

Jeremiah 1:4-10

For it is God which worketh in you
both to will and to do of his good pleasure.
Do all things without murmurings and disputings:
That ye may be blameless and harmless,
the sons of God, without rebuke,
in the midst of a crooked and perverse nation,
among whom ye shine as lights in the world.

Philippians 2:13-15

All the prophets had the same vision, whether Isaiah, Jeremiah, or Paul. It is God that works in you. It is *I*, the Lord, that puts the words in your mouth.

God, Ever-Present

The message of the Bible is that there is a God. This God formed you before you were in the womb. Before you come forth from the womb, God is your Creator. If it were not for that truth, you would have no right to expect perfect health through God. As God created the heavens and the earth, so he created your body, and that is why the Bible says that God will quicken your mortal body.

God gave you your body, and your body is the temple of the living God, so yet in your flesh you will one day know God. You will know the harmony of God, and this will all come to you by realizing that *I* in the very midst of you will never leave you or forsake you. So it is that when these trials come, when you go through the forty years of the wilderness, you will not be overwhelmed; when you go through the deep waters, you will not drown; when you go through the flames, they will not kindle upon you, if you will always remember that God in the midst of you formed you, maintains and sustains you, and by the grace of God you are free.

You will learn to let the Lord speak to you within you. Not once do you talk back to God; not once do you tell God what you want; not once do you complain to God; not once do you tell God that you fear; but always in acknowledging any problem of the moment, you turn realizing:

> Whithersoever I go, I know God goes. In "the valley
> of the shadow of death," [3] God goes with me.
> Through hell, God goes with me.

It is that which enables you to face your problems until they are not problems any more. They are the opportunities that are given you to surmount every obstacle in order that you may come to the realization of this God, ever-present, always available, infinite in power, love, and grace.

Taking the Yoke of Mankind

One day when you are ordained to heal the sick and comfort the mourner, you may have to go through a world of infinite troubles, and sometimes it is wearisome. Often the Master had to go away to be by himself, sometimes forty days, with the weariness that he took on from those who were pulling on him, but always he came back refreshed and ready to take up the burden again. Whose burden? Not his! He had achieved his spiritual freedom. He took upon himself the burdens of the people who were being misled by their church; he took upon himself the burdens of those who were crushed by the weight of the Roman Empire. He sought to bring them their freedom, and some of the very ones he was trying to bless and free turned on him.

It was not only Judas. It was those who were willing to cooperate with Judas and all the other Judases: those who were willing to doubt; those who were willing to misunderstand; those who were willing to believe that he wanted to wear a crown for his personal glory. Be assured of this, nobody will ever wear a crown serving mankind. More likely it will be a cross. If any such person gets a crown, it will be in the worlds to come, not this.

You who take upon yourself the yoke of mankind, service to God through man, need every ounce of God-power, every ounce of support from those on the path. You will hear the Lord speak in your ear and say, "Go this way or go that way. Go to my people. Go to the nations of the world. Carry this word of Life." You will do it, and you will have problems, but you will not have fear. Sometimes the weight of the problem will be more than you can carry, but you will not have to fear. You will know why you are doing it and you will know that regardless of the earthly scene there is a spiritual one.

Those Who Have God Have No Fear

You have burdens to bear: family burdens, community burdens, tax burdens. So be it; bear them. If you have to cry a little about it, cry a little; but do not fear, for *I* within you am with you and *I* will not leave you or forsake you. *I* will be with you until the end of the world. This is the message of the Bible. This is what the Bible is saying from Genesis to Revelation: there is something called *I. I* will never leave you or forsake you. *I* knew you before you were in the womb. The Lord knew you. And He knew you all the way through from the womb to the tomb. Do not fear. Grumble and complain once in a while. It is sometimes good to do that; it gets it out of your system. But do not fear.

Regardless of your problems, you can bear them, and if you

go down under them for the time being, that is all right, too, as long as you do not yield to fear because in fear you lose your God. God does not lose you, but temporarily you lose God, and life can be a terrifying experience to a person who loses his God, a person walking up and down this earth wondering when the next accident is going to come along, the next germ, or the next something or other. When you have God, you do not even care when the next bomb comes, because even that cannot separate you from the love of God.

There is God, and It is ever available right where you are in any and every circumstance. It is available when you are going through the fire, through the floods and the hurricanes, even when you are going through "the valley of the shadow of death." Do not turn your back on God because you have a problem. That is the time to reach out more than ever, remembering that "it is God that worketh in you both to will and to do of his good pleasure." So when the going gets very tough, that is the time to relax—not the time to tighten up. That is not the time to get fearful; that is not the time to get tense and strained: that is the time to relax and realize, "I don't do this; it is God that worketh in me."

A Divine Purpose to Life

Fear stems from the belief that there is no God and no purpose to life on earth. What you must learn is that there is a purpose; there is a reason why you were formed in the womb. Do not ever think for a moment that it was an accident or that your parents were responsible for it. They were not. They were only the instruments used by God to bring you forth into this world. Never think that your parents created you or that you have created any children. You have never been the parent of a child. You have only been the instrument through which God delivered His child to earth and that not to your purpose and your glory: for His purpose and for His glory.

As soon as you wake up to that, you begin to realize that you were not created for the things you thought you were. There is a divine purpose in your being here, but you will never discover it as long as you think you are a man or a woman created by your parents. If that were the case, then all you could ever hope to be is a human being with human limitations.

But the moment you begin to understand Jesus' admonition, "Call no man your father upon the earth: for one is your Father, which is in heaven,"[4] and to know that your parents were merely instruments used by God to put you here on earth and that if you are a parent you have only been an instrument used by God to bring your children here on earth, you will begin to understand the meaning of a divine purpose. You may see, too, why it is that in sixty-six books of the Bible, there are hundreds of individuals who heard the voice of the Lord, and that made them prophets, saints, sages, seers, and saviors. As misguided a person as Saul of Tarsus was, a persecutor and killer of Christians, even he could hear the voice of the Lord and become the great Christian disciple.

Nobody can ever be so unworthy that he cannot be lifted up to the heights. How? By a recognition that there is a divine Creator. From Genesis to Revelation, you read about the Creator who created man in his image and likeness and created the heavens, the stars, the suns, and the moons, the oceans and the fish therein. Even the fish were created for a purpose; even the birds were created for a purpose. Everything on the face of this globe was created for a purpose, a divine purpose.

When you understand this, then you will see how you can come into a relationship with all persons because now you do not treat them as human beings. You look upon every person and thing and say, "Just think, the same Father that created me for some divine purpose has created you, too, for some divine purpose." Then you will understand that we all have a common heritage, a joint heritage, a united heritage. We are not separate beings, nor is anybody over and above us except the Lord that formed us.

Problems are not problems when you have God. They are just experiences you meet as they come to you. You jump over one hurdle and on to the next one because you and I are divine beings with a divine message and a divine purpose.

God Is Calling: Do You Hear?

God has spoken into your ear and given you a mission. This is true about everybody, although there are always those who have ears and do not hear and the blind who have eyes and do not see. They do not know that there is something inside them capable of speaking to them, ordaining and commissioning them as prophets, saints, and seers, and upholding them as they go out about their work, sometimes with fainting footsteps, but upholding them nonetheless.

To know the will of God and to hear the voice of God means above all things developing the practice of having many periods of solitude every day, going into the inner sanctuary. The first argument that comes to most students is, "I have no time. Others may have, but I haven't." Of course, it is not you saying that at all. Everybody has twenty-four hours in every day, so there is no person in the world who has more time than another. Everyone has the same amount of time—twenty-four hours in every day. It just depends on what use is made of those twenty-four hours.

I wish you could see what my life is like. You would enjoy it. I sit way back inside myself looking out through my eyes. You would be surprised what I see out there in that detached sense, the funny things I see and the funny things I hear. Not knowing that I have a sense of humor, you do not know how often I chuckle inside. As I travel the world, sometimes I hear students say that they cannot afford this book or that book, this class or that class, or they cannot afford a tape recorder or a tape recording. They cannot afford this and they cannot afford that; they haven't time for this, and they haven't time for that. I just sit back and laugh and laugh inside, and then I look around at all the beauty salons and the prices they charge and the time they consume.

When people say that they have not time to attain this dominion, do not believe it any more than when they say they cannot afford this or that. It is entirely a matter of how they wish to use their time or their money. People can afford anything and everything that they truly want, and they can find time for everything. It is not a question of time or money: it is a question of which thing a person values most highly.

You have to retrace your footsteps to the Father's house through the many periods a day in which you determine to take mastership of your clock and not let your clock tell you that you do not have enough time. You tell the clock that you have twenty-four hours of time each day and sixty minutes in each of those twenty-four hours. Count them: twenty-four times sixty, and see how many minutes you really have out of which to set aside these periods of meditation, even if it is only ten minutes before the rest of your household is awake, if it is five minutes after the men folk have left the house, if it is five minutes before sitting down to that lunch or that dinner, or if it is ten minutes before going to bed.

If you would use just those few minutes when you awaken in the middle of the night, you would soon find that you are developing a capacity to be still, to be quiet, to be listening. Nobody can tell you whether it will take one week to receive the first intimation that something has happened or whether it might not be, like in my case, eight months, eight months of more than a dozen periods set aside every day for meditation. Still it took eight months before I had the first response. But then I had the second one a week later, and I had the third one probably two weeks later, and then a fourth one, one week later, and then gradually two in one week, and then eventually one every day.

Destroying the Four Temporal Kingdoms

It is not the whirlwind; it is not the hurricane or the storm that expresses God: it is the "still small voice."[5] It is the gentle Christ. And that brings us to that final and most important word. From Genesis to Revelation, there is God, the presence of God, the might of God, the power of God, and the strength of God. But as you come near the end of the Bible, from Matthew on, you begin to learn a new word, and that word is Christ. It is a word that you have to take just as It is without any explanation, without any appeal to the reasoning mind to understand It, for the more you try to understand It, the less you will have of It. The more you can accept the term, the Christ, without question, without any desire to analyze It or understand It, the more of It you will have. The more you try mentally to probe Its meaning, the less you will have.

Scripture tells of the four temporal kingdoms using metals as a base, meaning the forms of matter, and that these four temporal kingdoms will be destroyed. And how are they to be destroyed? By a rock that is carved out of a side of a mountain without hands,[6] and this rock is to fall on the four temporal kingdoms and crush them. Even though it is not possible to analyze such a statement or reason it out humanly, still spiritually you can discern that there is That which is invisible and infinite, which takes from all material form its power, revealing that the power is not in the form but in the invisible Creator of the form.

That statement does not mean that the world will do away with gold, silver, brass, or atomic energy: it means that the Christ will take the destructive elements out of the forces of this world and govern them. An example of that is electricity, the use of which the mind of man governs and harnesses for man's purposes. Now the world is witnessing atomic force being harnessed, not to destroy man but to serve man, and so the destructive force will be removed, and atomic energy will be a gentle little lamb governed by the mind of man. The mind of man which has no material form and yet is the avenue of our intelligence will harness atomic power, and eventually atomic power will be just as gentle as electricity is when it is properly hooked up, not a destructive element, but a constructive element, a servant of the mind of man.

Gold, which today dominates and rules man, even buys men's souls. There is not a day of the week when men and women are not selling their souls for gold or for the equivalent of it. Gold, or its equivalent, money, which governments are using in attempts to conquer each other, will someday become just a pliable little thing in your fingers that you yourself will use and over which you will have complete dominion. It will never be able to buy or bribe you, but you will use it, not hold onto it, but transfer and use for a constructive purpose.

Gold will be so tamed that one of these days it will be nothing more nor less than an instrument for your use—like streetcar transfers that have only temporary value, and which you transfer. So it will be with currency of all kinds: it will no longer be power. The power of the Christ will crush all power out of money as a force, and it will become a tool, merely a servant that you can mold to your use.

Through the Christ, Man Attains Dominion over Form

One day all forms of matter will literally be under our feet. Germs—there will be no fear of germs for they will have been conquered. For many years the Eskimos were subject to tuberculosis to such an extent that the medical facilities of Alaska were inadequate to care for those who came under this scourge. Then a law was passed permitting the Eskimos to be brought down to the States for treatment. Within three years, tuberculosis had been so conquered that the sanitarium used for this purpose was given up because they had no further need for it. Those germs had been subdued. They were no longer the master of the Eskimos.

So it will be with all material forms. Disease will not master mankind, and neither will the calendar. The calendar is one of the worst enemies of mankind there is. Every time a person tears off a page, it is like tearing up part of his life: there goes yesterday, and fewer tomorrows are left. But that will not always be true. A calendar will some day be man's friend, and he will be in such complete control over time and the passing of time that time will have no effect on his mind or body whatsoever.

Furthermore, instead of man dying with either disease or old age, when his time comes to go into a higher experience, he will make the transition same as a child goes into the adolescent period and the adolescent goes into the period of maturity. But that will not be while the calendar has power over men—or germs or money or bullets or bombs. It will be when man has dominion over the four temporal kingdoms, when through the Christ, through the gentle Spirit, the "still small voice," man will be able to say, "Thus far and no further. You can have no power over me unless it comes from the Father."

Within you, there is this gentle Christ which may be called the "still small voice," or "the voice of the Lord." As you develop the capacity to hear it, it is your dominion over everything on this earth, above the earth, or beneath the earth, the dominion that was given to you in the beginning when you were the image and likeness of God. Man was given dominion over everything in the earth, everything in the sky, everything in the waters beneath the earth, and everything in between, and the means of that dominion was the voice of the Lord.

The voice of the Lord came to Adam and Eve. The voice of the Lord came to Abraham, Isaac, Jacob, and Moses. The voice of the Lord gave Moses dominion over those difficult experiences in Egypt. The voice of the Lord gave Jesus dominion over food, over disease, over death itself. The voice of the Lord does all these things. "He uttered his voice, the earth melted,"[7] that is, the four temporal kingdoms melted, all problems disappeared, and all that which had dominion over man was overcome.

Not Death, but Transition

The day will come when that rock carved out of the side of a mountain without hands, that gentle Christ, that Spirit of God within your consciousness, will give you dominion over every element of human life, including time, age, and death itself. Should the time come when you want to pass out of this plane of existence, you will, not through being pushed out through some horrible disease, but just by gently easing yourself out and into whatever experience lies before you, because there is a higher experience that lies ahead of all of us.

When your appointed time comes, it will be a transition into a higher plane of consciousness, one in which you will be freed of all human ties, human responsibilities, and human obligations. While you are here, you cannot shirk these, but the day will come when you will be released from them into the ability to walk your own way in the footsteps of God.

You will do this through this thing called the Christ, or the spirit of God in man, the gentle Presence, or the "still small voice." Call It whatever you will; It is within you; It is available to you through an inner hearing; It is available to you through an inner seeing.

The Power of the Voice

The Voice, the word of God, is quick and sharp and powerful, and when that Voice utters itself, the earth melts; the whole four temporal kingdoms of the earth melt. I have seen all forms of sin and all forms of disease melt away when that Voice spoke within. I have seen all kinds of human wrongs made right through It. I have seen things that you cannot imagine come to pass just by that same Voice that gave me these Bible passages for this lesson. It is the voice of God, and It is called the Christ. It is the gentle Presence; It is the calm; It is the inner assurance or tranquility. Until you have It, you are nothing. Until you have a contact with It, within yourself, you are nothing. You are just an aging human being. But when you have That, you have made contact with the living waters, with the streams of life that renew and restore. It is that which gives you command over the four temporal kingdoms.

It will not allow money to be your master: It lets you be master over money so that you can command whatever is necessary for your legitimate needs. It will not allow the body to master you forever. The Christ enables you to master not only your own body but, as in the experience of Jesus and present-day spiritual healers, even to govern the harmony of the body of those who come to you for help.

It you ignore It, if you refuse to make your contact with It, if you do not have the stamina to stick with It until It does take over your life, you will have to do it in the next life. Some day or other, you can be assured that every knee is going to bend, every head is going to bow to God. So if you put it off in this lifetime, do not think you can continue to put it off into the next, or the next, or the next. Some day you are going to have to look a clock straight in the eye and realize that you have twenty-four hours of sixty minutes each and "Brother, I am going to use you. You are not going to use me: I am going to use you." Then it is that you will find those five and ten minute periods when you can seat yourself and say, "My faith is not out there in the whirlwind, in the fire, in destruction. My faith is in the "still small voice" within me. When He utters His voice in me, the earth of problems will melt away. I am going to learn to be still. I am going to learn to listen."

Some of you may report in a year or two that you have not done it yet. All I can answer is, "What difference does it make? You still have another year or two, or three, or five." You do not have to be in as much of a hurry as you think. It is not the youth who have done all the great things in life. It is some of those who did not attain until they were far beyond the status of youth, although Jesus did his mighty works in his early years and passed out of this plane of existence when he was thirty-three, already having completed his work on earth. In 1875 when the first edition of *Science and Health* was published, however, Mrs. Eddy was fifty-five years of age, and she completed her work at ninety. When *The Infinite Way* was published, I was fifty-five years of age. Everything is not done by youth.

If you cannot learn to meditate effectively this year, keep at it next year and the next. Eventually you will learn, and when you do, you will have overcome the four temporal kingdoms in some degree. No longer will this world have complete mastery over you. You will have begun to have mastery over many things of this world, little things to begin with, greater as time goes on.

There have been great composers at eighty, great inventors, great artists. Time means nothing. Years mean nothing. Longevity really means nothing. There is no particular credit in living to be ninety or a hundred. Many persons have done their work at thirty or forty. Longevity is not everything. The developing of maturity is, and if you attain your maturity at thirty, that is fine; but if you do not attain it until you are sixty, that is good, too. If you do not come into the fullness of it until seventy or eighty, that is good, too, because you have forever.

Nobody is ever going to become extinct, and the degree of your spiritual development when you pass on determines where you begin on the other side.

Each one of us was known before we were in the womb: we were known to God; we were ordained. Before we were in the womb we were made a prophet unto God to serve God's purpose in one way or another. Every day ask yourself the question, "Am I showing forth God's glory? Is there something more I need to know?" Then learn to listen and listen and listen until that Lord speaks to you as It spoke to every character in the Bible: Moses, Joshua, Elijah, Elisha, Isaiah, Jesus, John, Paul.

It was not just one favorite that God had. The Bible is full of those favorites. God spoke to King Solomon; God spoke to David. As hard a man as David was in many ways, nevertheless, he was able to hear the voice of God, and certainly Solomon heard the voice of God. The whole Bible is a testimony to the fact that men who were willing to hear it could hear the voice of God.

Ruth heard the voice of God; her mother-in-law heard the voice of God; Esther heard the voice of God; the mother of John the Baptist heard the voice of God; Mary heard the voice of God. Everyone who attunes himself can hear the voice of God, and hearing the voice of God he is the servant of the most High, an instrument for His use. And without that, he is nothing, nothing.

The Word of Life

The Bible has the word of life. The Bible and the truths of the Bible, however, will not do anything for you in a book. They will not do anything for you even after they are incorporated in my writings. These Bible texts begin to work for you only after you have moved them out of the books into your consciousness, dwelt on them, pondered them, as if they were seeds that you were planting in your mind, and then let them take root and grow as you water them and fertilize them each day by renewing them through pondering and thinking upon them.

The message of the Bible is that you are nothing *of yourself.* You are nothing except as the Lord speaks in your ear. You are nothing except as the Lord holds you by the hand. "The earth is the Lord's, and the fulness thereof,"[8] so you cannot claim even a possession; you cannot claim even your bank account; you cannot claim the cattle on a thousand hills. "The earth is the Lord's, and the fulness thereof." As you learn to release everything in that way, all of a sudden you hear it bouncing back at you with "Son, . . . all that I have is thine."[9] Then you understand how you have everything while having nothing.

Your Father is glorified in that you bear much fruit. If you are not fruitful, if you are not successful, healthful, harmonious, God is not glorified. God is not glorified in turning out failures; God cannot be glorified in turning out dead mortals. God is glorified in the harmony of your being, just as God is glorified by the beautiful light in the stars, the sun, and the moon. God is glorified by the fruitage on the trees, and so God is glorified in the fruitage that you bear.

The message of the Bible is that there is a God, and that without this God you are nothing. In the conscious remembrance of God, you are fulfilling the purpose for which you were created.

Across the Desk

It almost seems as if the original meaning of the Christmas season has been lost in the commercialism that has developed to the point where most people think of Christmas only in terms of the gifts given and received, and most with the emphasis on the receiving aspect of it. The origin of gift-giving is in the story of the gifts that the wise men brought to the Babe they were seeking. It was their homage to the Christ which the infant represented.

So let our gift-giving be our symbol of our recognition of

the Christ within those to whom we give, and then it will be a true pouring forth of love. The symbol itself is not important: it is the loving that is important. Then we can drop anxious thought for what we shall buy and let our love pour forth in simple ways, but ways which will always bless. To do that is to feel the joy that must have been felt by those who recognized the Christ in that Babe on that first Christmas Day.

About the Series

The 1971 through 1981 *Letters* will be publised as a series of eleven fine-quality soft cover books. Each book published in the first edition will be offered exclusively by Acropolis Books and The Valor Foundation, and can be ordered from either source:

ACORPOLIS BOOKS, INC.
8601 Dunwoody Place
Suite 303
Atlanta, GA 30350-2509
(800) 773-9923
acropolisbooks@mindspring.com

THE VALOR FOUNDATION
1101 Hillcrest Drive
Hollywood, FL 33021
(954) 989-3000
info@valorfoundation.com

Scriptural References and Notes

CHAPTER ONE

1 Isaiah 2:22
2 Luke 15:16
3 Psalm 22:1;
   Matthew 27:46
4 Exodus 16:3
5 Matthew 3:17
6 1 Kings 19:12
7 Psalm 23:2
8 1 Timothy 3:16
9 John 12:32
10 Matthew 18:20
11 1John 4:4
12 John 8:58

CHAPTER TWO

1 John 18:36
2 I Corinthians 2:14
3 Romans 8:20
4 Romans 8:17
5 Matthew 4:20
6 John 8:58

7 Revelation 3:20
8 Isaiah 54:17
9 II Corinthians 3:17
10 Isaiah 45:2
11 John 14:2
12 John 8:32
13 John 10:30
14 Luke 24:49
15 Isaiah 2:22
16 John 5:31
17 John 5:30
18 John 14:6
19 Hebrews 13:5
20 John 4:32
21 John 11:25
22 Luke 15:31
23 I Kings 19:12
24 Job 23:14

CHAPTER THREE

1 John 19:11
2 Matthew 6:6
3 Genesis 1:3

4 I Samuel 3:9
5 John 10:10
6 Matthew 6:10
7 Acts 10:34
8 John 4:32
9 Genesis 18:32
10 Philippians 2:5
11 II Corinthians 3:17

CHAPTER FOUR

1 II Corinthians 3:6
2 John 6:26
3 John 2:19
4 Psalm 139:8
5 Psalm 23:4
6 John 10:30
7 John 4:32
8 Revelation 2:17
9 John 6:35
10 Matthew 24:44
11 I Thessalonians 5:17
12 Psalm 91:1
13 Galatians 6:8

CHAPTER FIVE

1 Job 23:14
2 Psalm 138:8
3 I John 4:4
4 John 5:30
5 John 14:28

6 John 14:10
7 By the author, *Living The Infinite Way* (New York, New York: Harper and Row; 1961) pp.20, 21
8 Ibid., p. 21
9 Ibid., pp. 21,22
10 Luke 15:31
11 Joel 2:25
12 I Corinthians 15:31
13 John 9:25
14 Matthew 4:4
15 Matthew 6:11
16 The New English Bible (Great Britain: Oxford University Press; Cambridge University Press, 1961, 1970).
17 Luke 24:29
18 John 6:50
19 Luke 17:21
20 Robert Browning
21 John 4:32

CHAPTER SIX

1 Matthew 9:6
2 Isaiah 26:3
3 Proverbs 3:5,6
4 Matthew 6:7
5 Job 23:14
6 Psalm 138:8
7 Isaiah 45:2

[8] Isaiah 2:22
[9] Exodus 3:5
[10] John 18:36
[11] John 16:33
[12] John 19:11
[13] Acts 20:24
[14] I Peter 2:2
[15] I Corinthians 2:14

CHAPTER SEVEN

[1] Romans 8:14
[2] Romans 8:17
[3] Psalm 127:1
[4] Isaiah 2:22
[5] Psalm 146:3
[6] Isaiah 45:2
[7] I Corinthians 3:16
[8] I Corinthians 6:19, 20
[9] John 8:58
[10] Revelation 21:27
[11] Joel 2:25
[12] Matthew 25:40
[13] Zechariah 4:6
[14] I John 4:4
[15] Job 23:14
[16] Psalm 138:8
[17] Psalm 19:1
[18] II Chronicles 32:7,8
[19] Galatians 2:20

CHAPTER EIGHT

[1] Matthew 4:4
[2] I Kings 19:12
[3] Luke 17:21
[4] Psalm 127:1
[5] John 5:30
[6] Joel 1:4
[7] John 8:11
[8] Matthew 22:37, 39
[9] Matthew 26:52
[10] I Kings 19:18
[11] John 5:30
[12] John 14:10
[13] Matthew 6:11
[14] John 6:35
[15] John 1:14

CHAPTER NINE

[1] Acts 3:6
[2] John 12:32
[3] Genesis 18:32
[4] Matthew 18:20
[5] Mark 1:24
[6] Joel 2:25
[7] Isaiah 2:22
[8] Luke 15:31
[9] John 10:10

CHAPTER TEN

[1] Joshua 10:12,13
[2] John 18:36
[3] Habakkuk 1:13
[4] Matthew 5:39
[5] Revelation 21:27
[6] II Corinthians 5:4
[7] I Corinthians 15:31
[8] Matthew 9:24
[9] John 11:43
[10] Psalm 17:15
[11] Psalm 102:27
[12] Hebrews 13:5
[13] Matthew 28:20
[14] I John 3:2
[15] I Corinthians 6:19
[16] I Thessalonians 5:17
[17] II Corinthians 6:2
[18] By the author
[19] John 10:30

[20] Luke 15:31
[21] John 12:45
[22] Psalm 42:11
[23] Psalm 23:4

CHAPTER ELEVEN

[1] John 8:11
[2] Isaiah 2:22
[3] Luke 15:31
[4] John 10:10
[5] John 8:58
[6] Alfred, Lord Tennyson
[7] Philippians 4:13
[8] Galatians 2:20
[9] Matthew 5:38
[10] Matthew 25:40
[11] Isaiah 45:2
[12] Matthew 14:27

CHAPTER TWELVE

[1] John 12:45
[2] Luke 4:18, 21
[3] Psalm 23:4
[4] Matthew 23:9
[5] I Kings 19:12
[6] Daniel 2:34-45
[7] Psalm 46:6
[8] Psalm 24:1
[9] Luke 15:31

Joel Goldsmith
Tape Recorded Classes Corresponding to the Chapters of this Volume

⌒

Tape recordings may be ordered from

THE INFINITE WAY
PO Box 2089, Peoria AZ 85380-2089
Telephone 800-922-3195 Fax 623-412-8766

E-mail: infiniteway@earthlink.net
www.joelgoldsmith.com
Free Catalog Upon Request